NEURODIVERSITY:
A Humorous and Practical Guide to Living with ADHD, Anxiety, Autism, Dyslexia, The Gays, and Everyone Else

by Barb Rentenbach
and Lois Prislovsky, Ph.D.

A Mule and Muse Production 2016

Contact Information
www.muleandmuseproductions.com
Email: info@muleandmuseproductions.com

Printed in the United States of America
First Edition: January 2016
Published by Mule and Muse Productions with Sojourn
Publishing, LLC

ISBN: 978-0-9883449-1-4

Contents

Dedication
by Barb

Atlas Hyder Patterson is an exceptionally radiant soul. Pat (October 26, 1920 – June 10, 2014) is pictured here with his classy wife Wilma and treasured cat, Hyde (star of the children's book *Little Boy* a Mule and Muse Productions coming attraction.) I reach out and touch Pat's physical body with extra joy and appreciation, as we both know it is for the last time. Pat moved on and now he does not talk out loud either, but our friendship is alive and well. God I love OLD friends! I begin this book with a poem written by Betty Tankersley, which appears at the end of Pat's book, *Little Boy*:

THE END

Tonight I looked upon two words
I never thought I'd see,
I shook my head and looked again
And they looked right back at me.
The words I saw just said, "The End",
Finis, goodbye, adieu,
Should I be glad or am I sad
That my assignment is through?
I have learned more about a cat
Than I think I'll ever need,
But this I'll tell you anyhow,
At least I had to read
So goodbye to you, Little Boy,
And to your Master too,
Wage on your war; go see the King,
And don't let any fleas bite you.

bjt

Dedication
by Lois

Rachel Prislovsky's gift is uplifting others. My grace-filled Mom taught me to love play and work. I am also forever grateful to Charles (aka Dad) and Rachel Prislovsky for consistently demonstrating how to live the loyal, compassionate, and tender marathon of marriage. As wise seventy-eight-year-olds do, Mom is pictured here enjoying the inflatable obstacle course at our annual Pink House Thanksgiving Celebration.

Special Thanks

Chad Dougatz (cherished producer & brother)

Jennifer Ho Dougatz (priceless marketing guru)

Dr. David Haines (best dressed and most dependable editor)

Dr. Ty Heath (perpetually over the top wife and "non-paid" friend)

Carol Holloway (compassion filled, patient personal attendant)

Andrea Lyles (outstanding and loyal Office Manager)

Barbara and Mike Rentenbach (stalwart board of Trustees)

Jerry Richardson (kindhearted boyfriend & GIANT encourager)

Tom Bird Publishing (loving, top-notch project managers)

Kristin Toussaint (photographer, videographer, and heartographer)

Eli Prislovsky Warwick (Best Boy - by far)

Emma Willmann (our favorite gay, dyslexic, ADHD, anxious comedian)

Jeri Yarber (enthusiastic and dedicated personal attendant)

Preface
by Barb Rentenbach

"Autism is my prism, not my prison." Me

My last book was about shattering pity with purpose. This book is about creating equality with perspective.

Courage and connection are needed to give all gifts and is our collective purpose. Courageously with you, B

by Lois Prislovsky

"Psychology need not be devoid of humor to be of service." Me

My learning is usually filtered by what strikes me as funny. I left those often-irreverent perceptions in these writings, knowing that some readers will not share in the humor and will think me unprofessional. Hopefully, "real me" sharing will make understanding these issues easy and entertaining to those who would not ordinarily read books written by serious Ph.Ds. Besides, the serious Ph.D. market is flooded, and seriousness does not always suit my intention to serve by helping others feel they fit in, so that they may soar less encumbered.

May these imperfect words lighten your path – as they have mine.

Foreword
by Comedian Emma Willmann

As a dyslexic stand-up comedian, with ADHD, anxiety—and a strong case of homosexuality—I was surprised that what I related to most in this book was not any of these "descriptors"; rather, it was how Barb uses her differences to get through airport security. (I travel A LOT – talk about practical implications . . .)

While my differences are different from Barb's (Thank God—explaining biting and smearing feces to my roommate would be tough. It is a small apartment. I know it is Harlem, but still). I am a big fan of her utilizing her traits—both those that society commends and condemns to her advantage.

This book is filled with hilarious, refreshing, and touching stories about using differences in ways you would never imagine and are not always PC. But more importantly, the takeaways about LIFE are profound. The best, hardest, and most dynamic forms of the human condition are highlighted as the means of cultivating a more authentic relationship with yourself and in turn yielding compassionate and productive friendships based on your most spirited identity. No hiding: just cultivating, mastering, and embracing.

My first introduction to Barb and Lois was when they reached out about doing their podcast, Loud Mute Radio. Nothing seemed different about this podcast request, until the follow up email noted that the host, Barb, was an autistic mute, and unable to communicate verbally.

Of course! I thought, makes perfect sense. **Just my luck.**

Like guilty teens spotting mall cops, my thoughts sprinted in all directions. I considered a Loud Mute Radio TV interview perhaps on location in Narnia and pictured trying to lip-read with Barb and radio silence. Are mutes like mimes? Will Barb wear gloves, whiteface, . . .? Maybe the show is for hipsters?

Then I finished the email. I am not sure about any of you with ADHD, but part of mine involves jumping around when reading emails, along with a wandering mind (. . . who invented the Oreo?).

The email went on to say the verbal portion of the interview would be conducted by her gay psychologist, Lois.

An autistic mute and her lesbian therapist, doing a podcast? Of course!

Maybe next a blind man and his transgender accountant can lead treasure hunts for the Discovery Channel. However, as fate would have it, meeting Barb and Lois really was **just my luck.**

Barb and Lois urge you to treat yourself as your best self - to ensure that that is what you become. And also, the all-important: to treat others as THEIR best selves. Accomplish this NOT by hiding your differences, but embracing them for the best in you and the world. The key is acknowledging and working to understand what makes up your neurologically diverse brain and THRIVING in its complexities.

They are brilliant, bizarre, friendly, and sometimes biting. Barb and Lois are Yin and Yang respectively. Their differences complement each other and their interactions establish harmony and wholeness that creates – a Mule and Muse Production if you will.

What are your differences? What is in your neurological make up that currently poses a problem, but could actually offer relief? A benefit? Instead of banging our heads against the wall (which gives me crazy non-PC images of helmet-wearing readers), we may gently guide ourselves to understand the difficulties that come with our neurodiversity as traits that actually produce our greatest strengths. For example, if you have ADHD, sure it's hard to find your keys sometimes (wait, OMG these are not even my keys) but there is no denying the strengths it provides. Too often we just consider what makes it harder and don't take the time or care to recognize what makes it incredible.

Now, celebrate your neurodiversity with compassion, humor, and everyone else! Goodie - Jennifer Lawrence...hey, about those Orcos...am I out?

My ADHD is getting out of hand, I'll go put it to good use somewhere else, and you read this inspiring work!

Dyslexically yours,
Emma Willmann

Like riding a bike, the benefits of neurodiversity once learned are never forgotten. In Tennessee, children under 18 are required to wear a bike helmet while riding an actual bike. Pimp hats are sufficient for bike riding idioms.

Introduction: Who we are, What we do, and How we do it
by Lois Prislovsky

When you treat someone as their highest self, you help them become that. Barb taught me that. We started with presumed competence but moved up quickly. Barb says she is "disguised as a poor thinker," so I treat her as a brilliant thinker. And that is how Barb shows up day after day – most of the time.

As my wife Ty says, "Barb is easy until she is not."

When Barb is easy, my day goes like this:

Early morning, I let the dogs out, imploring Matthew Beagle to save his pre-dawn baying to all rabbits for a more reasonable hour. I then drive son Eli to school. Next, I brew Ty prescription-grade French press coffee, the mere aroma of which cures my ADHD for about three hours – precisely what is needed because here comes Barb. With her personal attendant (PA) escort, Barb makes the twenty-five-foot trek from her front door to our back kitchen door. In these parts, only pious pamphlet pushers ring the front bell. Barb is selling connection so she walks right in – no need to knock, as she is one loud mute.

From 9 am to noon, five days a week, Barb plops down on her favorite church pew in our dining room – underneath the most comically bad ceiling rendition of Michelangelo's "The Creation of Adam" – and gets to work for three hours straight. With one of my fingers touching her back to jump-start her past apraxia, Barb types what she wants to accomplish that day and in what order. She usually chooses to work on her writings, radio show, emails, conference calls and social media.

At noon, Barb's PA returns and takes Queen B to lunch. Her afternoons are filled with a variety of scheduled activities. For example, Barb pays her bills on line with her house manager; researches history, philosophy, guests for her show; practices independent typing with an ASD specialist; works out with her hottie personal trainer du jour; has bi-monthly massages, and regular dates with her boyfriend, friends and family. Barb would want me to be clear that she schedules several hours of "chill time" in the late afternoon when she is not required to be "on." During that time, Barb "re-fuels in her autism" and mentally plans for the next day. **This chill time step is key**, for it is when she goes back into her "autism." To do this, Barb gets someplace safe and comfortable, like her bed or front yard swing, and puts her body on autopilot. Barb explained to me that once she sets her ill-wired physical body aside, she mentally becomes extraordinarily agile and creates imaginative connections. Like many individuals with autism labels, Barb thrives with a structured schedule. The next morning, Barb enjoys her Cheerios and relaxing bath. Barb perfected her bath time ritual years ago and has the instructions typed out for training new PAs. Her attendant washes all Barb's body quickly but thoroughly, and then playfully rinses her hair by dumping a plastic beach bucket of water over her big head. The next part Barb does solo and is for mature audiences. She soaks for exactly 15 minutes. Her attendant then returns to dry and rub Barb with medicated lotion (for psoriasis, not autism). A little deodorant, dressing and teeth-brushing assistance, and Barb is ready to "change the world a lil' more to my liking." (Picture the pampered grooming scenes from Eddie Murphy's character Prince Akeem of Zamunda in the movie *Coming to America,* with a little less dialogue and a lot less melanin – and you get the idea.) Barb then returns to our pink house to peck out her fresh perceptions.

For me it is like Christmas morning. It is fun helping Barb open the exciting gifts of her mind each day.

After Barb, I get to work on Psychoeducational Network business and prepare individually for my diverse afternoon clients, and then fetch Eli from school.

When Barb is not easy… it's less like Christmas morning, and more like a human flesh-biting, clawing, squealing, and jump-out-and-grab-you, shitty Halloween.

The days Barb struggles with outbursts of aggression and uncontrolled ferality occur much less often than they did when we started working together, almost fourteen years ago. These days Barb's explosive outbursts are rare… but no less exciting. It usually happens after Barb is exposed to negativity, or over-stimulated, or overwhelmed with change or responsibility. We just recently weathered the perfect storm where Barb experienced all of the aforementioned and was mostly unable to produce quality work for several weeks.

Barb and her team know that her grueling days will pass. If we give Barb time and safe space to chill and process… she will eventually regulate and type about her experiences to help herself and others.

Meanwhile, her PAs keep scrubbing poop from Barb's fingernails, teeth, sheets and everywhere she touched when she gets into such an overwhelming daze that she smears and tastes her feces. We all dodge her grabs, pinches, and hair pulls. We all try and calmly redirect our brilliant Barb when she smashes her own arm into her open, biting mouth with such force that she breaks the skin. When Barb bites this hard, she usually bears down and pushes out a slow, universally clear squeal declaring her agony – often followed by her echolalic phrase, "I don't know. I don't know."

None of us know when she will break through, so we do our best to keep her on schedule – but we play it day by day. Even on difficult days, she usually comes over and tries to type. Sometimes she is able to create and communicate. But it is not easy. The other day, after a self-biting binge, Barb jumped up and charged me like a matador on the final pass. I literally ran around our long dining room table, but not before I rescued her prized Mac Air from a certain crushing murder. After a few laps, Barb settled and I said, "It is hard to work with you when you are like this." Barb typed, "You are telling me. Keep going! I have to feel this to know this."

Eventually she broke through her "autistic fog," and she was able to complete this book and resume her podcasts.

It is not easy being Barb. Why does she keep going? I think Barb knows for now that her job is not supposed to be easy, as she types, "My process is my story." When people understand what she goes through every day to be the best she can be – it is humbling, and it inspires formidable gratitude. I tell Eli to slap me if I ever complain about my life, because Barb does not complain – and as Barb typed on Jennifer Ho-Dougatz' show called "Big Girl Panties," "I do feel successful. I honestly believe I am doing the best I can with what I have… and I have plenty."

It is not easy working with Barb. Why do we do it? Because most days, Barb is a profoundly gifted and generous thinker, and the embodiment of patience and perseverance. Our last book took ten years to write, and this one we finished in four years. We are making progress. I stand by the ten words in which Zoom Magazine asked me to describe Barb – complicated, imaginative, dedicated, spiritual, wise, honorable, grateful, witty, and PATIENT.

Barb says she is "disguised as a poor thinker." Perhaps I am disguised as a neurotypical thinker – maybe not, as my exceedingly comfortable shoes are rather obvious markers – plus spell check can only do so much – and look – a squirrel. (I am literally standing up and moving as I type this.)

This book is our truth. It is designed to help folks lighten up and move on and be themselves on PURPOSE.

I may be criticized for sharing so much about my own self when covering ADHD, Dyslexia, and Homosexuality, as psychologists don't do that. I am okay with that as I often enjoy things that middle-aged white women with lots of diplomas don't do. (My forty-eighth birthday party this year was playing airsoft wars in an 80,000 square-foot warehouse made to look like Fallujah with twenty-five of Eli's teenage buddies and my redneck Dad friends. I know this sounds weird and painful, and lets face it – Donald Trumpy racist, but it was crazy fun. Barb's brother and nephew played, but Barb did not come… something about singing lessons.) Barb will not catch flack for typing about herself because she "has a doctor's note for being an autistic mute," plus everyone wants to play her if her story is made into a movie because it will be easy to remember the lines.

She uses her "get out of jail free autism card" more often than one might think, but those are her tales to tell. (Do ask her about eloping drunk and naked in the Bahamas. It's a doozy.) To her credit, Barb is generous with that particular advantage of her disadvantage and can be counted on to help her less-than-completely-declared buddies sail through customs like Saudi diplomats when needed. Once, coming back from Jamaica, our friend "J" was about to be detained by M-16-

toting Federalizes who were not born yesterday. So Barb grabbed J's arm to pull him through security, behaving as his confused and petulantly disabled charge perhaps needing urgent bathroom assistance. Before that distraction even had a chance to work, she iced the cake by pulling her pants down in the metal-detector arc. When sweaty officials began to excitedly bark about the chaos, Barb strategically leaned slowly near each official face and touched it ever so gently, leaving her capris down a bit longer to seal the luniacal deal. Thrown off guard by personal space rapes – and with none of this being worth their pay grade – in unison, the customs guys abdicated all responsibility and hastily escorted our gang of five shifty, giggly Americans through. Barb knows how to take one for the team. (Warning: These stunts are performed by professional autistics. Mule and Muse Productions is not responsible for any harm or injury resulting from neurotypical re-enactment attempts.)

This book is about playing your position well. We intend to present two characters who are friends and business partners – who have two very different skill sets but have found a way to connect and lead joyous and productive lives – not in spite of our "disabilities," but because of them.

We hope some of you equally qualified weirdoes will enjoy the stories, and relate – and maybe even alter – your perspectives by thinking about how such obstacles and disadvantages can lead to excellence… or at least a few more authentically rewarding lives.

Disclaimer

Our format is NOT politically correct. Also, I think the best book about neurodiversity is Thomas Armstrong's *Neurodiversity: Discovering the Extraordinary Gifts of Autism, ADHD, Dyslexia, and Other Brain Differences*. But Barb is funnier – so we throw our book into the ring, hoping our contribution will warm up popular culture to neurodiversity. Plus, demonstrating that we are all legitimately of value is good for the economy.

I am not even an Opus Dei flavor of Catholic, but typing on my own is so laborious, I often get enraged and bite myself and pound my arm into my teeth to amplify the pain. Then loving personal attendants like Jeri help me refocus and continue my work. Trying B

Chapter 1
Crack Smoke and Pawnshop Mirrors
by Barb Rentenbach

"Our perception is like a ray of light falling on a plant – it makes it more visible, nourishes it, stimulates its growth. Think of how many talents and qualities in everyone that are not fully manifest because they are not seen." Piero Ferrucci in *The Power of Kindness*

I type on my own now with several different people, but it is painfully slow and it took literally years of tedious practice to accomplish. In the past, using the hand support of others while I typed was my only way to communicate, which brought considerable suspicion about me being a plus-size marionette.

I wrote in copious detail about how I learned to type solo in *I Might Be You: An Exploration of Autism and Connection,* and I have posted many videos of me doing my thing on our web site at www.muleandmuseproductions.com. I even have multiple YouTube videos showing off my sentience, one letter at a time, for good measure. Unfortunately, I included very few cats or trampoline accidents, so the Barb Rentenbach channel has not gone viral.

In this book, I no longer sing the same song proving myself as a blind, deaf, mute – no wait, that's Helen Keller. I sing from my Golden Ratio heart and let the word chips fall where they may, hoping to take ASD understanding mainstream with humor, scholarship, and fresh perspectives.

Great books speak across time, as they have no expiration dates – but Dads do. So I start this book with a chapter I wrote for Father's Day. My Dad, "DD" (Dearest Dad – I am a big fan of monikers especially ones that are easy to type) also calls me DD, which sounds ironic, as all the women in our family would visibly make lamentable strippers. But he means "Darling Daughter." Our bond has always been limitless love. You won't catch me complaining about my allotment in life. Present perspective is what I have to give, and it is the skeleton key of life. (DD already has the key to my heart… and the city, as he pretty much built both.)

In this chapter, I offer the opportunity to think differently.

This is a horrible tale, perhaps more suited for Halloween than Father's Day, but one must live in the present – and this story is about the present of being present. The names have been changed to protect the not-so innocent.

I had to fire my live-in house manager who, I discovered, was embezzling my grocery money to feed her drug habit. She also took my prescription nausea meds, which I need occasionally as I have a persnickety gut (like so many autistics) and I often overeat, which has nothing to do with autism and everything to do with heavenly carbs. As a bonus, most of my jewelry is now on sale at all the best pawnshops in Knoxville. The gig was up quickly. You see, as my tattletale thighs attest, I think about eating a great deal. I noticed that the bottoms of the grocery receipts were torn off by hand – no longer the work of practiced cashiers, slashing with register shark teeth, so beautifully designed for such separation work. And that night, I needed my Phenergan and was told, "You are out." Bullshit. I saw six in the bottle last week. The next morning, at my first opportunity to type, I sent the following email. I should note that when I wrote this email, my Smiling Shrink (SS) supported my hungry hand. Nobody but my non-verbal autistic self who is disguised as a poor thinker, and the poor-thinker house manager, knew about the Phenergan or the untidy receipts. Mel was my day-shift personal attendant at the time, so I copied and included her as a heads-up so no one would try and blame her. Below are the actual emails I saved in my AOL "drugs2" folder. This was not my first drug rodeo.

From: Barb Rentenbach
To: "Donna"
Cc: "Mel"

Sent: Fri, Oct 28, 2011 8:33 am
Subject: concerned

hi donna. as you know mel and i are concerned about you. i don't want to lose you. i love you in my life. at this time, this email and conversation is just between you and mel and me with ss of course holding my hand. here is the deal. no more being late. it is my pet peeve. no more taking my medicine. you are a wonderful person, especially when you are clean and sober. please let me know if there is anything i can do to help with either of these requests. lastly, all credit card receipts need to be intact and not torn. okay donna? please work with me and know that i will work with you. nobody is perfect, but some things just won't do. thank you. concerned b

Donna responded to this ultimatum with contrition, promises to make amends, sincere gratitude at being given a second chance AND me not telling my VIP parents. Problem solved? Yeah, no. What addicts say and what addicts do is politician-like in the discrepancy scale. It wasn't two months later that her chronic tardiness resumed, I was "out" of meds again, and gnawed receipts abounded. Only Donna and I were privy to these details. Again, as soon as I got a chance to smash my nail-bitten finger on those freedom keys, I sang like a federally protected jailbird. I retrieved the warning email saved for just such an occasion and brought my parents into the mix. Time for Donna to look for another job (one not requiring a recommendation from this previous employer).

Sent December 23, 2011
no more. donna, as you can see from the letter below that i sent you on october 28th 2011, i have been thinking about this for some time. in fact, i saved all such correspondences in a file labeled "drugs2" as i feared this day might come. i have been through this before my friend.

3

i know the game and it ends now. my hope was the meeting with mel, you, me, and ss would scare you straight as i know you do not want to lose your job or reputation. i really want to work this out with you, but am prepared to move on. i know you have continued to take my phenergan. i know you have lied to my staff and family many times. i know you are chronically late especially when relieving mel in the am and pm. i know you are in big money troubles. i know you have fraudulently used my credit card many times. no more. you are better than this. so am i. i wont be taken advantage of. please understand i want to work with the real donna. she is beautiful inside and out. let me know what time and support you need to deal with these issues. thank you for receiving this with love and introspection. life is a process of gaining wisdom and becoming better versions of ourselves. lets get to it. love, b

To be fair, I did not sniff out the pawnshop part as precious metals and stones are less on my radar than abundant string cheese and bountiful pantry pretzels. After the second confrontation, authorities discovered a thriving Barb resale network.

Some folks knit. I make AOL drug folders. Want to hear about my first? Like rubbernecking a wreck, you don't want to hear about how someone took advantage of a cute autistic mute – but it is hard not to look.

That which we call a Rose is the lady I had before Donna as my house manager. ('Tis but thy name that is my enemy.') Rose also got the ax. She got so messed up on crack and meth that she started lying most of the time and got me to my appointments late. OMG, I hate being late. I don't speak, but I can reliably say, "She is not here" or "Just a minute" as timeliness is next to Godliness and that is where I choose to be. This one had an even darker flair, as Rose often slipped me drugs to make me sleep so she could party. I am a cheap drunk, so it took me some time to catch on to this crack hat trick. But I damn sure noticed when her drug dealer crusty skank boyfriend moved in one night. I may be a tranquilized quiet type, but Hell no! I squawked as soon as I had sea legs. I did not even wait till my official typing time. I typed this out with the hand support of my personal trainer, Joe, at 9 am, two hours before I rolled in to SS's office. Mortified, Joe told

SS right away; she plugged me in to my lifeline email, and justice was served. SS went with me to my tasteful West Knoxville condo, and we found dozens of mini-firepit burns on Rose's mattress in her room next to mine. Apparently, we dodged a Richard Pryor kinda sizzlin' on many occasions. With all the roofies I was being fed, aliens could have had all manner of probing experiments with me… but the crack heads seemed less ambitious.

Does this true-crime log prove I am smart? Maybe. However, hiring druggies does seem ill advised. It does show, however, that I am present.

Practical Implications:

1. Presuming competence is a good way to show respect… and not get fired.
2. If you have the precious fortune to experience limitless love, BE GRATEFUL and replay that emotional luxury like "The Little Mermaid" video in an understaffed daycare.
3. Our aut department teaches listening well. In my case, not being able to scream well-constructed arguments forces me to really listen before carefully choosing my hand-pecked words. This diplomacy skill was obscured by my first rage-communication techniques: biting, clawing, kicking, grabbing, and hair pulling. My Ultimate Fighter career was not successful, so I finally moved on (just in time, too – have you seen the bruisers in my weight division?). When you confront someone, be genuinely open to hearing her side and finding a solution together. Give her the benefit of the doubt. Respect is not possible without listening. Ferrocci, the author of *The Power of Kindness: The Unexpected Benefits of Leading a Compassionate Life*, reminds us that "true listening only happens in silence" and "true understanding requires pause and commitment." Not listening leads to the perception of unfair treatment, and thus "enemies." History teaches this, as Germany did not feel they were heard and felt that the Treaty of Versailles was unfair. So they revenged the world. Making vindictive caregivers, who know my security code, is not a good move for anyone – especially an unarmed mute.

Healthy adolescent development is a time of role transitions. Eli (15) and our buddy Evan (16) regularly contribute to the family business with invaluable teen consultations, an embarrassing amount of technology support, on-air performances, lots of heavy lifting, and other serious adult business as shown here.

Chapter 2

Teen Angst and Cow Farts
by Lois Prislovsky

A family recently flew me across the country to help their teenage son. Like many adolescents, he struggles with anger, anxiety, depression, prevarication, social skills and loneliness. Winston Churchill advises, "If you're going through hell, keep going." Of course, Winston was not dealing with troubled teens, just world war and a diaper-wearing vegetarian, but he is right – keep moving forward. That is precisely the action-oriented path this family and others are navigating to get through hard times with their teens. All parties can cooperate to understand more and move forward, with positive change on each issue.

What works for Aretha Franklin also works for teens: R. E. S. P. E. C. T.

R = Reminders. Like modern day matadors, thinking it is probably time to find other work, some things are obvious. When the tone of family communications needs to change, everybody knows it. Parents and teens can all agree they want to be treated with respect during discussions. Adolescents may want "fewer commands and more conversation." Parents may desire less contempt and defensiveness. Each person can change the tone by doing his or her part. Every act of good will and cooperation will pave this new road out of an adversarial rut. One family found a private joke reminder to help them stay on track. Whenever somebody (one of the parents or the troubled adolescent) noted behaviors that were not congruous with their common goal of giving and receiving more respect, one would utter the phrase, "**cow farts**." The more ludicrous or humorous the cue word or phrase, the better. **Like a warning light on a car dash, the idea of this cue is to get your attention and motivate you to do something different. The developmentally positive, common goal is to engage**

collaboratively, not reactively. Psychology need not be devoid of humor to be of service.

E = Empowerment. Healthy adolescent development is a time of role transitions. The relationship dynamics that worked when these young people were children no longer serve the goals of the parents or the adolescent. Time to change. Give the young person time to think about how he or she would help their own child with the same issues. Twenty-four hours is usually enough time to avoid the impulsive "I don't know" shut down answers. Parents, be genuinely curious about what your teenager thinks. Such curiosity communicates safety and a deep level of caring on your part, and promotes introspection rather than rumination on the part of your teen. Young people want to be respected for their mature problem-solving abilities. It is a powerful and natural intrinsic reward. Give them the opportunity to be a big part of their own solutions. Some ideas may be as helpful as silent letters, but others may be insightful. Validate practical suggestions with non-patronizing praise and implementation.

S = Sarcasm. Research shows that anxiety is often the precursor to depression and an array of behavioral problems. With teens, sarcasm often helps the medicine go down, so in the sarcastic language of indigenous adolescents, here are a few tips for anxiety:

1. Starbucks. Nothing stimulates flight-or-flight-or-freeze-or-collapse response like a pounding heart. If you want to experience high anxiety and perhaps even full-blown panic attacks, go for the Grande. And if you are a huge anxiety connoisseur, order a Venti, red-eye. A Trenta, black eye (two shots of espresso in regular drip coffee) is theoretically possible, but survivors are likely an urban myth. Legend has it that old-timey comedian Robin Williams got the closest as he rode out the tachycardia, irritability, and sweats, only to become an excessively hairy cocaine addict five sleepless days later. (Warning: This stupid idea may also cause facial tics, compulsive hair pulling, skin picking, irritable bowels,

insomnia, and other way-fun "I told you so" symptoms preached by old people.) This particular tip may also be used to speed poverty onset. Enjoy that drink!

2. Cram. Want to vamp up test anxiety too? Stay up all night, cramming. Nothing depletes Dopamine faster than messing up your sleep cycle. With less Dopamine, your memory and attention will suffer, but that is nothing compared to the loss of motivation and drive you will feel at exam time. Lack of sleep has also been shown to desensitize Serotonin pathways, so your brain will scream to your mind, "You are not safe or well!" Test freak out much?

3. Play video games by yourself forever and ever and ever. Who knew the "relaxing" path of least resistance could actually increase anxiety – but it does, in oh so many ways. For one thing, gaming stimulation, especially one hour prior to bedtime, increases insomnia, which starts that Dopamine dumping. Also, because in-person social skills need to be practiced, especially during adolescence, you can expect to lessen your ability to communicate and connect with others. Dating will suck more. Building relationships with everybody should become more awkward, which will lower your success in most endeavors. The crazy good news is that doing something so easy (hours and hours of solo gaming) will actually make your life much harder, which of course will increase anxiety.

P = Presents. Give non-monetary gifts to each other daily. Research shows that caring for others increases resilience to stress. When we connect lovingly with others, our brain rewards us with Oxytocin (aka the "cuddle drug"), a powerful hormone which acts as a neurotransmitter, increasing feelings of optimism and self esteem. Studies are showing that naturally produced Oxytocin may be effective in reducing anxiety and depression. One of the best ways to score Oxytocin is to hug a drug dealer... oops, scratch that – the sarcasm part is over. HUG a loved one!

Many adolescents experience anger because they are in pain and do not know what to do about it. It is often safe to blame parents, since peers and others would not tolerate the angry focus. Like candy cigarettes, this is a terrible idea for multiple reasons – and better strategies must be learned and practiced. Giving can help change that pattern of negative thinking. Oxytocin has also been observed to increase generosity. Most teens love their parents, but they do not often let parents know they are important and appreciated. Daily gifting by teens and parents can bring the focus back to what is working. We all have something to give. Our gifts are of different currencies – such as emotional, physical, mental, etc. – but all are of value. The exquisiteness of giving your strengths is that it does not deplete, but actually builds, your strengths. Practicing considerate giving is vital for learning the social-skills exchanges necessary to be successful in the adult economy. For example, upon returning from a vacation, without being asked, our towering teen went to the luggage carousel, collected all our bags, carried all to the car and loaded it. My scrawny, tired self did not lift a finger. He was proud to do it. We were proud to accept. He said little, but communicated expertly.

E = Exercise. Clinical trials show that regular exercise works just as well as or better than medication to reduce anxiety and depression. The effects can be long lasting. One vigorous exercise session can help alleviate symptoms for hours. Consistency is important, and may significantly reduce anxiety and depressive symptoms over time. Moderation is necessary. Becoming a Michael Phelps will not solve all your problems (for a variety of reasons – please see Dopamine depletion and jail time). Consistent exercise for thirty minutes to an hour a day for healthy teens should be sufficient to jump-start neurotransmitters to help the individual feel well, and motivated to take positive action on life problems.

C = Compassion. One mom was so furious about what she perceived as her son's "manipulative behaviors" (cutting) that her tone was blocking the start of the new style of communication that the family all agreed they wanted. But, this wise mom was part of a seasoned couple who strengthen each other, so she knew the power of flexibility. She then chose the emotion of compassion at the first family meeting. As a result, anger did not permeate the discussion, and the goal to establish one or two points of agreement – using open and respectful dialogue to establish a pattern of collaboration – was accomplished.

One can get practiced at choosing emotions, especially when the options are mutually exclusive. For example, one can't be anxious and relaxed at the same. An honest reflection about your own teenage years may help sustain a compassionate state.

Compassion is welcome currency everywhere, which sure beats bitcoin. As Warren Buffet said, bitcoin can be an effective way to transfer money, but so is a check. Compassion checks are easier to write than you may think. Plus, the feds don't chase down teens who take it.

T = Thank you. Say it authentically and often. This healing phrase is in a teen's control, and it empowers both the giver and the receiver. Neale Donald Walsch said it perfectly: **"The struggle ends when gratitude begins."** Thank you for your patience with your teenager's learning process.

Like not blaming others, some things take time to learn, but then you know it for good. Which came first – the chicken or the egg? Chicken is the correct answer. True story. Wanna hear another? **Grateful people are happy.**

B Team At Hangar Studies in NYC recording our new audiobook and Loud Mute Radio show. Carol Holloway (Personal Attendant), Chad Dougatz (Producer), Lois Prislovsky (Idiot), Jeri Yarber (Personal Attendant), and One Loud Mute (Centered).

Chapter 3

The Cure

by Barb Rentenbach

"Quiet people have the loudest minds." Stephen Hawking

I study history, as it helps me know what people are likely to do. The present is a sensory overload, so I prepare for it by studying the past.

The past is stable, which gives me time to consider it. Luckily, my 504 plan specifically allots me more time. My favorite edification is historical biographies, as they serve my Golden Ratio design preference to examine the micro in order to learn of the macro. "Those who don't know history are doomed to repeat it," wrote Edmund Burke. Mr. Burke, that is what I am counting on. I learn from patterns.

Today, I got my history fix from a Harvard-trained lecturer, Rufus Fears. I realize his name is more suited for my anxiety chapters, but scholarship demands I cite his real name rather than the pseudonym "Ed U. Cator." Harvard never did admit me – something about my non-existent application, severe autism, ataxia, apraxia, and an overrepresentation of rich white girls. Fortunately, this gal had the $69.99 price of admission for Great Teaching Course DVDs. This class was entitled "The History of Freedom," concerning Lord Acton's writings (1834-1902).

Like Acton, I had an unusual education. The formal and useless part of mine took place in a series of special-needs classrooms, plastered with fading laminated posters of the alphabet and hand-washing instructions. I heard bad jazz renditions of Velcro schedules, recrudescent nagging, and the loud clicking of 504,910,816 seconds until graduation at age 21. Once sufficiently aged, I received a Special Education Diploma, which let potential employers know that I can be counted on not to cause too much destruction. This educational moratorium also saved lives. This was no life for me or Smother, but that school time probably gave us enough space to avoid murdering each other. And now I know my ABCs.

Like Lord Acton, I was not admitted to Cambridge either. Acton was not accepted because he was Catholic. I am Catholic too, but perceptions change and Cambridge no longer rejects Catholics; however, being disguised as a poor thinker is a tried-and-true, automatic "NO, THANKS."

Both of our grandfathers saw to it that we got a good education anyway. We each started by hiring German tutors: Doellinger for Acton, Elke for me. We studied Plutarch and the classics. Germans are all about record keeping, and they both had us writing about what we learned. "Learn as much by writing as by reading," instructs Lord Acton. (I agree, but he said it first.)

The central theme of Lord Acton's life was the idea of conscience. He wanted people to be educated and have the liberty to follow their own conscience, not to be ruled by the all-powerful majority. Or is that my theme?

Either way, we both amassed essays, notes, and volumes of writings: he in his vast library; me in three-ring binders that SS keeps in her office, with the overflow under her bed. The difference is that Acton never wrote that book.

I have finally sat down to write books. I have SS keep all my early stories, research discussions, session notes, and musings. In 2007, SS started saving it electronically. I am having her print it out, not because of a tree vendetta, but because it helps me see the forest in the trees.

Words take so long for me to birth; reclaiming them as needed is a gift.

Being heard may be as close to helping to cure all that ails ya as one prescription gets.

Ariane Zurcher, Autism Advocate rated #1 on the Internet by Dr. Oz, and eloquent voice of me in the audiobook version of *I Might Be You: An Exploration of Autism and Connection*, heard me. Then she loaned me her voice. That selfless gift started a healing snowball.

I was then heard again by thousands of listeners on David Alpern's nationally syndicated radio show, "For your Ears only." Before some poor clerk from the DMV (Department of Miracle Validation) at the

Vatican calls my number, please know I am still mute. So my Smiling Shrink, SS, dutifully presented my words. The experienced producers, knowing that mutes are reliably bad for ratings, authorized this Milli Vanilli-esque substitution.

Like a drooly Labrador bounding back pitch after pitch from Lake Loudon, SS kept care of the words I threw into her smiling mouth, and dropped them when and where she knew I wanted.

Hearing my words in the audiobook and on the radio healed something in me. It was more than scratching an itch. It was surgical, immediate healing, like setting a bone or removing a tumor. It is a lasting cure.

Like me, like you, like "THEM," poetry is also best heard. Two of my favorite lines from Derrick Brown's poetry are, "Dumb as a bomb on a boomerang" and "kiss like you couldn't beat cancer."

We are all each other's cure. God cares about us all through us all.

Please say this out loud – as I am borrowing your voice to be heard, and God is watching if you deny an autistic mute such a simple request: *"I will not be as dumb as a bomb on a boomerang. I will listen like I couldn't beat cancer."*

May you also be heard. Thanks for hearing B.

Practical Implications:

1. Listening adds value to what is being said and to the person who says it. When one hands over this double coupon, one buys the peace of silence. It is a perfect transaction.
2. Great Teaching Courses are a value, perhaps especially for non-normative communicators.
3. "Learn as much by writing as by reading," Lord Acton and Queen B
4. Being heard is best. Give that to someone.

Tennessee Snow usually melts by noon, so we chose to skip typing this morning as other construction and demolition projects took president. Ty Heath, MD assists with hypothermia monitoring and "bubble" placement. Barb assumes a supervisory role, but only because her snow toilet did not make the photo as it could not bear her weight (despite her engineering pedigree) nor her screams (despite her mute status).

Chapter 4
Play – Easy as ABC
by Lois Prislovsky

"If you want to know what your thoughts were like in the past, look at your body today. If you want to know what your body will be like in the future, look at your thoughts today." Deepak Chopra

Take a minute to think of a few of your best memories. Were they in moments of play? We often feel most alive and connected in playful times.

Play is practicing a sustained state of relaxed alertness, and it is the chicken soup (or matzoh ball soup for those of you who know the value of a dollar) of mental and physical health. Children are masters of this fully present state of effortless learning and creativity. We are wise to take note – get out your purple crayons.

Stewart Brown, M.D., in *Play: How it Shapes the Brain, Opens the Imagination, and Invigorates the Soul,* reminds us that play "shapes the brain and makes animals smarter and more adaptable. In higher animals it fosters empathy and makes possible complex social groups. For us, play lies at the core of the creativity and innovation."

Play is all natural, free, and legal in most states. It's as easy as ABC:

A. ADAPTABLE.

Adaptability is key to survival and well-being. Children are usually more flexible and resilient than adults. Why? The answer is child's play.

Science confirms that we learn almost effortlessly through play, as more brain regions are activated. Then the brain releases hormones – and here come the good drugs that many folks would risk orange-is-the-new-black fashion to get: Norepinephrine, Oxytocin, and Serotonin.

But our culture is changing, and our helicopter parenting and over-scheduling has taken not just some of the fun out of play, but also many of the benefits.

As Fareed Zakaria artfully presented in *The Post-American World: Release 2.0*, Americans have traditionally produced a globally disproportionate number of entrepreneurs, inventors, Nobel Prize winners, and risk takers because our students were allowed to be bold, think independently, communicate with and challenge authority, fail, and pick themselves up.

Traditionally, not everyone got a trophy.

Tim Elmore's most recent book, *Artificial Maturity: Helping Kids Meet the Challenge of Becoming Authentic Adults*, expands on this insight as he illuminates this generation of young people as "overexposed to information far earlier than they are ready and underexposed to real-life experience far later than they are ready."

Elmore contends that because our children know they "know a lot of data and other virtually acquired information," our kids often come off as arrogant and confident on the outside, but are often anxious or depressed on the inside because self-awareness is developed through real-world life experiences. It is our job to help them learn to fail.

Play is a great teacher.

I got the opportunity to design and run our son's middle school (sixth, seventh and eighth grade) obstacle course for field day the last three years. I did this because as a psychologist, I know our children need experience taking calculated risks and experiencing real-life problem solving. Plus, having the authority to make hundreds of kids jump over swimming pools of green Jell-O is straight-up fun.

The course was challenging, highly competitive, and only relatively safe – shocking to these overprotected children. And they LOVED it.

After each team completed the event, I empowered the slightly battered victims with the genuine question, "Is there anything we should change before the next group?" "NO!" was the resounding response every time.

The course was diverse, so it favored no particular body type. Speed and strength were helpful, but so was creativity. Some kids figured out they could save energy at the start by making an alliance with their opponent to hold hands and jump off the elevated log together, rather than struggling to wrestle the other child off. (What? I put pads on the ground... on one side; the wise fell in that direction.)

Clever teamwork choices could also significantly increase one's chances at success. On the ball-pummel section, contestants were required to catch just one large Pilates exercise ball before moving on to the Hippity Hop downhill. The huge balls were thrown from about fifteen feet back by their own teammates, and the other team who were waiting their turn to compete. Here is where the serious play got interesting. Ingenious strategies emerged, ranging from cooperative, lofty throws to a variety of sabotage techniques. Ball withholding was my favorite, as it was the most brazen and aggressive – it is not easy to hoard fifteen balls the size of most sixth-graders from twenty frenzied opponents.

However, as in life, perseverance was the true game changer. Everyone got tired, but those who pushed through unfamiliar levels of fatigue were able to somehow bang the pots and pans hung high in the "winning tree" to conclude their turn and defeat their opponent – earning a point for their team. Many popular, athletic Goliaths went down that day because persistent Davids wanted it more. Even when Goliaths got to the tree first and were already making their way up the thick climbing rope, Davids were not deterred. Some underdogs shook the middle-school giants off the rope (which was actually not the best strategy, as now the dearborated Giant was in hand-to-hand combat, and usually willing to pay the high cost of revenge). More successful Davids simply climbed right up and over the Goliaths, using them as steps.

Children want the opportunity to push themselves when it is not easy. Everybody spontaneously hugged, high-fived, or shook hands with their exhausted opponent. It was a great memory moment. And, yes, there was a clear winner.

Attitude is everything with obstacles. Everybody gets tired, but those who arise from suffering and adversity change the world.

B. BE PRESENT.

To quote from one of my favorite books, *Zen and the Art of Motorcycle Maintenance,* unlike traveling in a car where "You're a passive observer and it is all moving by you boringly in a frame. On a cycle the frame is gone. You're completely in contact with it all. You're in the scene, not just watching it anymore, and the sense of presence is overwhelming."

Why not be there? When I see parents sitting on the side at parks (trampoline, water, amusement, etc.), I don't get it. Okay, maybe I understand the amusement park, as something about being forty-eight years old makes me throw up after every decent ride and park food is expensive.

My point is that **you have to be there anyway – so be present**.

Let your mind go (irresponsible sounding but not), and play. Even if you are not good at it – especially if you are not good at it. **Graciously trying things that are hard teaches our children and ourselves volumes.**

Kids just let their minds go. They avoid stuckness and are much more open to new ideas. *Super Brain: Unleashing The Explosive Power of your Mind to Maximize Health, Happiness, and Spiritual Well-Being*, by Deepak Chopra and Rudolph Tanzi, beautifully presents how children are sponges for novel information and experiences, and that promotes neuronal growth. (There is a reason we do not see Alzheimer's in children – okay, that is not exactly it, but my point is related.) As adults, we too often are wet sponges too, saturated with our habits and established points of view. Child's play can help with mental and physical flexibility, leading to new brain cells and connections.

Play naturally encourages flexible and unique thinking. For example, my son and I love combining activities to maximize joy – like playing baseball while the batter stands on our roof. We use a rubber chicken projectile because it's fun – and it's easier on windows and passing cars.

When you play with your children, you connect. Talking is natural, and roles shift effortlessly – practicing both communication and the transition needed for eventual independence. When you are mutually able to enjoy a conversation about a rule loophole in Nukemball, a safe foundation is built. (Oh, Nukemball is a fascinating game I just learned at our son's eighth-grade graduation gathering. Please note this was not a party. Like a sandlot baseball game back in the day, word of mouth and a few texts (we are not Amish) let families know to bring their own food and drink and meet at a local park following the ceremony. No food signup sheet, scheduled activites, RSVPs, or permission slips... just child's play. Best memories were made.) Back to the game. Nukemball is played on a sand volleyball court – you pray. (I'm sure it can be played indoors or on grass but – OUCH!) It is similar to volleyball; however, you catch the ball and throw it over the net rather than hit it. The object is to get all the other team's players out by throwing the ball over the net and getting it to land on your opponent's side. If the other team fails to catch it, the player who touched the ball last or is closest to the ball when it hits the ground is out. Oh, and if you catch it with one hand in a feat of glory and inevitable body sacrifice, you bring your whole team back in.

Playing together leads to communicating together. **When you can talk about nothing with your children – the shift is easy and not awkward when it is time to talk about something**. Talk while you are playing, as that state of mind opens you both to being present and learning.

Shefali Tsabary, author of *The Conscious Parent,* writes that in the conscious approach to parenting, "children serve as mirrors of their parents' forgotten self. Those willing to look in the mirror have an opportunity to establish a relationship with their own inner state of wholeness. Once they find their way back to their essence, parents enter into communion with their children, shifting away from the traditional parent-to-child 'know it all' approach and more towards a mutual parent-with-child relationship. The pillars of the parental ego crumble as the parents awaken to the ability of their children to transport them into a state of presence."

C. CREATE

The state of play brings many Aha! moments. One may catch on to a rule or get a great idea for a new strategy – and this delights.

It is estimated that 80 percent of our thinking is done at the subconscious level, and we are only aware of our thinking 20 percent of the time. Being consciously immersed in play allows the mind to dance, free of thoughts, and that is when creative thinking is ripe. **When our mind is working on what we are not thinking about, our intuition and interconnectedness peak.**

Not all play has to be raucous movement. In fact, years of sitting still in a Baptist church taught me competitive breath holding, which I dutifully passed on to our son, David Blaine. (Kidding… our son is not yet Vegas Magic impressive, but is up to almost two minutes). Or, if I am billing by the hour, timed breath-holding play is also a fine technique to help ADHD clients practice mind-body control and being still.

Play just needs to be voluntary, freedomful, improvisational, and for its own sake. (If you took notes on that definition of play, you may need to start small – go to the mailbox while chewing gum only with your tongue).

Play fuels creativity. My friend Barb struggles with movement (even the Special Olympics said "sorry, no professionals"), yet she finds play abundantly. Poetry is not her normal writing mode, but one day after taking the playful opportunity to try a saltwater sensory-deprivation tank, she emerged refreshed and inspired to write:

floating
by barb rentenbach:

my cup of tea

bag o barb floats
in the warmth
as she has done through the ages
flavoring the surroundings
seeping out to experience dilution and the feel of molecular
movement.

notes dance through my leaves
bombarding is banned for the float

i go while mesh holds my place
in this fine china of purity
non porous walls warm and shield me from all else
while i explore my limits of self.

i am expansive but not limitless.
good to know.
bag o barb is pleased.
thanks for the cup
i bring my own tea"

Find your way back to the essence of play and you will happily
find yourself.

Lois is naked in the hot-tub because that idiot was freezing from a snow bath. I got in because I rarely miss an opportunity to hot tub or get naked. Hard to say why our office manager Andrea got in; but I let her know this is not what I meant by swinging.

Chapter 5
I Bit Her Till She Bled
by Barb Rentenbach

"The worst mistake anyone can make is to perceive anyone else as lesser." Andrew Solomon

When reading my bloody words, consider postponing judgment as we explore the power of writing. Oh, the heavy-set nuns seeking respite from sweat and tattletales in the shade loved to tell this one. Sister Manicotti told us that Pharisees brought Jesus a woman who had been caught in the act of adultery (Sister did not elaborate on that part), and they asked Him if she should be stoned as Law required. They were trying to trap JC, and he knew it, so Jesus took his time and wrote something in the dirt. They kept pressing Him. (You know how irritating folks can be.) Finally the Lord said, "If any one of you is without sin, let him be the first to throw a stone at her." We don't know what JC wrote on the ground – but I am telling you, it helped.

I am only able to peck out my imperfections because Sister Donna Williams went first. Her courage to plunge into fear after fear, exposing her vulnerable inner world to "the world," taught me it was possible. Those without advanced degrees in tenacity need not apply for this work. Luckily for me, this muse has my fair share of mulishness. But it still ain't easy. As I type this, I break every few seconds to bite my arm. It is not possible to touch letters with my left pointer finger and bite simultaneously because I use my dominant left hand to pound my right wrist into my open mouth and disciplinarian teeth.

In the same *New Yorker* article as quoted above, "The Middle Things: Advice for Young Writers," Solomon adds: "What I'd really like, in fact, is to be young and middle-aged, and perhaps even very old, all at the same time – and to be dark- and fair-skinned, deaf and hearing, gay and straight, male and female. I can't do that in life, but I can do it in writing, and so can you. Never forget that the truest luxury is imagination."

I am a big fan of luxury. I too consume and produce writing to know and be more.

But typing strong words is not the same as yelling. When was the last time you lost your temper, and let the angry words spew uncensored?

Feel better then, did ya?

What if you could not speak, and had to wait till someone helped you type to get your feelings out? Could you wait a few hours, a day, a week?

What would that be like to not be able to express your anger, injustice, or disagreement at the time? Would your brain sear? Could you focus on other things until you had the chance to express? Could you broker a deal with the Sandman to hide the facts from your unconscious jury so rest could be had? I do all of that. But, sometimes it is not enough.

Ruminations that I manage to blockade always try a clever detour; the boldest get through. Drunk with over-importance, these nefarious thoughts embed and overload my system. Once the threshold is reached, chaotic blackout conditions rule.

I am blinded by a familiar but despised plume of charred fog that surrounds and permeates my entirety. Balance and sentience are gone. I become fear, rage, and utter confusion. Nothing can be done until the surge is purged and lights shine again.

In the last three weeks, I attacked four people with biting, grabbing, hair pulling, and hitting.

One of those assaults took place when I was riding shotgun with my Smiling Shrink (SS), and my rage was so sustained I bit her arm through her sweater, tasted blood, and yanked her hair from the back of her head to pull her into me so violently I knocked the car out of gear and it went dead on the Interstate.

Has my autism gotten worse? I hope not. These days I am writing professionally as an autism success story.

Are my meds failing? I only take a quarterly depo shot and a pinch of Lexapro. Come to think of it, I do feel kinda pregnant and a lil' depressed about that... but that may be more due to the endless breadsticks at the Olive Garden, which I think I have convinced my new personal assistant (PA) is where I am to lunch daily.

The truth is, aggressive outbursts have always been a part of my autism.

The frequency of my aggression has decreased significantly over the years, as I have become able to communicate more efficiently and REGULARLY. I don't think I can report the severity of the attacks has waned. But to be fair, I bite my own self more than I do others. I find that makes me more popular.

I am not proud of this. I am working on it. I am writing on it. Writing about negative thoughts when and where I choose takes away their free rein. SS has me practice having these thoughts without action, to lessen their influence, as I regard them as more commonplace – and merely background noise.

I share these ferocious warts because I want my beloved autistic siblings to know they are not alone in imperfection. While we should all be eager to learn from many, we should save pedestals for no one.

I do feel successful. I do feel autistic.

I do feel. We all do.

With love,
trying B

Practical Implications:

1. Swing better, swing. I am not in the penitentiary today because I have a swing in my front yard and I know how to use it. Swinging re-balances my rhythm even better than my usual rocking. If rocking is sipping Beringer, swinging is gulping a double shot of Cuervo Gold. I feel relief immediately. In fact, I plan to return to my swing as soon as I finish this piece. Swinging does not make my sensory integration issues go away, but it is a temporary vestibular fix so that calm focus

may be had. I recommend quotidian swinging – no I.D. required.

"One tequila, two tequila, three tequila, floor." George Carlin

2. Try writing often. My hero Donna Williams knows this well, as she has published eighteen books and is still going strong. In *Everyday Heaven* (2004), Donna eloquently shares: "Through writing, all my unknown knowing typed itself out. It spoke to my conscious mind through my eyes as they read my words from the page. I had found a mechanism via which I could move preconscious unknown knowing into consciousness, and it made me feel whole and in control of my life, my thinking, and my expression."

   I too use writing to understand my own mind, and that which seems external to it. My knowing is sensory based. My sensory flames burn naturally. Writing language is not natural for me. Writing is gas on my fire of knowing. Like a good forest ranger, through lots of smutty trial and error, I learned to use this accelerant to control burns. Writing is very hard to do, especially when sensations are blazing. Daily scheduled writing allows one sensory fire to be processed at time. One fire is warm and illuminating. Multiple fires are chaotic and dangerous.

"Bitterness is like cancer. It eats upon the host. But anger is like fire. It burns it all clean." Maya Angelou

3. Core of discovery. I often write that I study history to know what is probable. I also study history to know what is possible. Consider Lewis and Clark's boundary mission, the "Corps of Discovery." They were able to circumnavigate Great Falls by the Shoshone Chief, Cameahwait connecting with his sister, Sacagawea, in Shoshone who then spoke to her French-Canadian husband, Charbonneau, in Mandan who then talked in

French to Jusseaume (another interpreter), who communicated to Lewis and Clark in English. Gifts were exchanged and everybody got what they needed.

You will discover you can find a way to communicate. Then you too will exchange gifts – and you may achieve your destiny.

Eli, Charles and Rachel Prislovsky and me at Huntington Beach CA. Seasoned Pollocks, Mom and Dad don helmets for extra beach safety. If we know our core, we are wise to build our vocations and VACATIONS around that.

Chapter 6

Know Your Self, Purpose and Boundaries
by Lois Prislovsky

"Courage is not about being fearless; it's about letting fear transform you so you come into right relationship with uncertainty, make peace with impermanence, and wake up to who you really are." Lissa Rankin, M.D.

Dedicated to John, a man who knew how to set boundaries. John, who was "overloved," and who funneled that love to help others grow:

A Georgia elementary-school bookkeeper, Antoinette Tuff, prevented a mass shooting by calmly being with the shooter in his time of pain and isolation. By being herself filled with love, patience, humility and focused intent on reducing suffering, Antoinette stayed fully with him as he changed his course to be a better person.

We may all be able to make such profound differences when we live our part. The trick is remembering who we are and what we are here to do. In *Let Your Life Speak*, Parker Palmer explains that to know one's vocation (from the Latin root "vox" meaning voice), or calling, one must hear one's own voice. In school we are taught to listen to so many in power and authority, but not to ourselves.

Today, I encourage **you to hear you.**

Know thyself.

Recall times that are characteristically you. Explore your feelings and thoughts associated with those moments. It may help to jot down adjectives about what you were like in those moments. Your familiarity is there. You will smile when you see it.

Here is an example that may get your wheels turning and build your self-esteem simultaneously, as odds are your moments won't sound as stupid as mine.

I tried to save the Devil:

I was about nine years old and lying in bed one night, letting my ADHD mind flit, as I had not yet discovered my beloved Heineken medication. With no alcohol, and my safe little life stuffed with Southern Baptist and Private Christian education, the full dose (I never missed a day – seriously, I got a plaque and everything), my thoughts turned to forgiveness and salvation. It occurred to me that if my crimes (maybe, more on those later after I Google "statute of limitations") could be washed away by simply politely asking Jesus, wasn't Satan eligible for the same deal? I was taught about the book of Revelations, and I assumed the Devil read the ending. This is not going to work out well for a lot of people and fallen angels. Surely the Devil does not want to go through with this either. So Lucifer, why not just apologize and ask forgiveness?

A simple solution to ALL the World's Problems? Perhaps… perhaps not.

I will save the ethereal yet palpable details of this mediation/intervention-with-an-unlicensed-counselor anecdote for another time. For now, it suffices to say that the Lord does protect children and fools, and often works overtime for those of us with the co-morbid condition.

The point is – I know this person. I **am** this person. At my best, I may be simple, bold, and helpful. At my worst – we will again save this for another time, as this statute-of-limitations stuff seems complicated.

If we know our core, we are wise to build our vocations around that.

My beloved, astoundingly complicated friend and business partner, Barb, wrote, "Know your part. Be your part. Play your part with pride and conviction."

Once you remember who you are, with adjectives, decide how to verb up the good – and clock in for work. In *The Art of Communicating*, Thich Nhat Hanh teaches that **compassion is a verb. So are you, if you are to be of service.**

If you are brave, brave this world. If you are simple, simplify. If you are brilliant, illuminate us. If you are genius, please fix my new iPhone.

Barb says, "God cares for us all through us all." In wholehearted living, all are needed. All are welcome.

Please be yourself... it is for the best.

And now some notes on setting boundaries, lest you do-gooders get burned out with all this mindful compassion.

Asking for what you need is brave. Asking for what you need is honest. When you know yourself, asking for what you need is as it should be.

Unlike the National Security Agency (NSA), I asked permission and was given the family's blessing to share the following information.

John was a client of mine I will never forget. He found a way to ask for what he needed. This was not easy, as John had exceeded his expiration date. John was not expected to live past the age of five – yet he hung on until age thirty-four, because as John typed in his deathbed message, "I am overloved."

When I first met John, he was in his early 30s. His prominent family got my name from another affluent family who were clients. His mother asked if I would make a house call, as their non-verbal son was dying because he was refusing to eat.

John was diagnosed with severe mental retardation and cerebral palsy. I am not sure a diagnosis of autism ever came, but it was clear to John and all those who had the pleasure of knowing him that the "severe mental retardation" diagnosis had also exceeded its expiration date.

From early childhood, John surrounded himself with books and magazines, and taught himself to read. Later, at age sixteen, he learned to communicate on a large keyboard with the use of a facilitator. (A facilitator is a person who supported his hand to lift it above the keyboard and provided resistance to the downward motion as John pushed down to choose each letter.) Facilitated Communication (FC) is a controversial technique. More information on that topic may be found in *I Might Be You: An Exploration of Autism and Connection,* as Barb Rentenbach uses the same process, but can now type with a variety of support people who provide a light touch on her back to help overcome her ataxia by helping to initiate movement.)

This house-call request was a quandary for me, as Barb was the only client with whom I performed FC. I was no expert in the field – nor did I wish to be. I worked diligently to get Barb to type more independently, to avoid authorship controversies and protect my reputation. But my simple, bold and helpful self came through, and I went to him.

John was frail and beyond thin – thinner than you are imagining now.

His sister was suspicious of me and whatever typing we did. She took her role as his protector seriously, and wasted no warmth or graciousness on me. But toward John, well, her committed love seeped out of her eyes while her gestures and heart slowed in reverence when she addressed or tended to him.

John did not welcome me. He exceeded that. He flopped his typing hand and whole self on me with the gift of complete trust, and confidence in my muleness, to get him where he wanted to go. He used all of his stamina to crutch on my warm hand, throbbing with health, to type what he wished – and it was a lot. John held my hand and typed for almost two hours. He typed personal notes as "Christmas gifts" to his family and staff. I cried often. He did not. He was focused, and he was used to being so uncensored and tender.

After he typed what he wished, John allowed me to converse with him, and we discussed his will to live and nutrition. He agreed to eat. Mission accomplished. Or like George W. Bush, so I thought.

About two years later, his mother called again. This time he came to my office, which was precisely how John wanted it.

The family was asking me to train John's staff to FC with him. I am no FC trainer or expert, but I was open to be of whatever help I could. The first session, John came in with his mother and his head nurse, whom I will call "Mary." John was still concentration-camp thin, but he had better color, and he was able to walk, albeit unsteadily, from one seat to another in my office.

He typed easily – very easily. In fact, I simply pinched the fabric of his fleece sleeve around his wrist to have his impossibly light arm hover above the keyboard, and he did the rest. He was able to answer "yes" and "no" and "true" and "false" questions on his own, with no fleece levitation support, by typing a "y," "n," "t," or "f." Below is an excerpt from John's first session note. (Our practice is known for having each clinician write detailed notes describing what was accomplished, and emailing it to the client and/or family within twenty-four hours, so that everyone may be on the same page and be part of the solution.) I see now that John was counting on this copious notation so that what he communicated would not get lost in translation. John also made sure to email some writings directly to specific people. He was very precise.

Excerpt from session #1:

The bulk of my support was simply helping John keep his hand raised above the keyboard. He was clear about his hand preference and the keyboard he wanted to use. John was candid and succinct. He does not wish to facilitate with any of his nurses and states it is an issue of trust for him. John is confident he "will be manipulated." John stated he would only FC with his sister, but explained there is no need for that as they "are of one mind." John demonstrated a keen awareness of the personnel issues with his staff, and related family dynamics. He maturely and compassionately listened to all opinions and initiated some solutions. John agreed to meet with me once a week in order to develop his independent typing skills and strength, while corresponding with his staff and family about his care and personnel issues. (The next part of John's typing is redacted for privacy.)

John closed with a clever depiction of some of the issues discussed this afternoon: "eggshells is the dance of my clan." I am looking forward to working with this refreshingly genuine young man.

It should be noted that John trusted and adored his head nurse, Mary, and was able to type with her support in our first session. But he chose not to type with Mary on issues of family dynamics, staff problems, or hard-to-hear thoughts that John shared about life and death. He was protecting her from others and himself, as much of what he needed to say was too painful for a loved one to hear. And Mary loved John.

John was increasingly in more pain at each visit. John wrote,

"hi dad john here with my weekly email address. it is more difficult than one can imagine being in this pain body of brittle pointlessness. but the alternative offering requires a ticket that is not yet valid for me so today i peck out portions of thoughts i must ask u to respect."

It took John eight sessions to communicate what he needed. Then he died.

This note and excerpt is from his last session note:

Dear _____ family:

I just learned John died last night. It is not possible to imagine the pain of your loss. It is my prayer that these words be of comfort to you. John _____ was a precious, powerful soul. He taught the grace of patience. He lived humility and peace. He wanted the world to know he was "here," and "all there," but he was content with connecting fully and tenderly with all who made the effort to know him. When he sat on your lap as a grown man, it was not an immature gesture, but a gift of the rarest kind – the embodiment of pure warmth and compassion. John shared his "love funnel" purpose before he went home. Thank you, John!

Please know that John's account is paid in full. Thank you for the pleasure of working with John.

Sincerely,
Lois Prislovsky

Here are our session notes for your family records.

John was ready to work as soon as he came in, and he answered some questions about taking the shots and expressed some of his worries of late. Then he asked me to plug him into the computer and he responded to several emails (two from his dad and one from his aunt). His writing was very smooth and accurate; he looked at each stroke with his peripheral vision. He was very calm and on task for the duration today. He only moved seats two times, and once was to sit on my lap and hug me in between emails. Sometimes the blessings of this job are outstanding.

(The rest of these session notes for that month were redacted for privacy.)

Below is another privacy-redacted, but otherwise unedited excerpt from one of John's emails in his last days:

my gut is in nots it feels like the liing is riped. raw pain yes. but thingshave changed. Yes ok (Mary) please pleaeee. no cancel b. i n I need your help to die. I am done with thisv body . yes true. But now I have nothing left to give. Just being loving takes too much energy. Mmmmmmadffffffffffffffffffffi don't want that job pity is no job it is a state of being in wabnt I refuse to be a wanting soul. I wish to be without form or want. I cant standb no I wont stand the negativity in myb homee. . yes my purppse is to center love . to gather giving so all may be filled. Get it/? I know u do but home life uis gettimg too petty to let me funnel the gifts of love. So I am sick and tired my funnel got stopped up. time is too valued by those with no peace I need a time lapse video. Ineed you to stop (name redacted) from going to people and telling lies Yes yes . the negativity is kkilling my spirit. I want to chew real food. And (name redacted) is no longer welcome at my home honesty and peace will not allow it. I must have a refuge in order to work my love cleaners.email this to my famiy but I am serious.

John set boundaries. He knew his purpose and was not afraid to hold people accountable, so he was free to be himself and do what he was on Earth to do.

In *The Gifts of Imperfection* Brene Brown's research supports John's wisdom and found that the most committed and truly compassionate people were also the most boundary conscious. **John and other precious practitioners of compassion teach us to protect our energy from being drained by that which does not serve our intent.**

John is a "love funnel." That is his identity and intent.

What is yours?

I close with a line from one of John's long emails concerning his care, boundaries, and purpose in life, "Dad, hang in tthere I will make u proud yet. In loving truth, john _____"

Whom do you make proud?

Simply yours,

Lo

"Muleness is not something you learn in school, but if you haven't learned the meaning of muleness, you really haven't learned anything." Muhammad Ali

My boyfriend Jerry and I cruise past Neyland stadium as soon it will be teaming with the Vol navy and thousands of orange clad football fans. We intend to miss the crowd, but little else. Sometimes what is expected is not what is needed. Sometimes it is best to go with your flow.

Chapter 7

Turtle Soup for The Soul
by Barb Rentenbach

"People may not remember exactly what you did, or what you said – but they will always remember how you made them feel." Maya Angelou

Donna Williams was the first autism success story I knew. She too was feral, mostly non-verbal, and disguised as an exceptionally poor thinker. Donna broke through her sensory overloads, communication roadblocks and fears to became a prolific artist, filmmaker, autism advocate, best-selling author, and happily married. In 2002, SS and I began working together, and we listened to *Somebody Somewhere* on two audiocassettes, read by Debra Winger, in 1994. (*Nobody Nowhere* was actually Donna's first international bestseller; *Somebody Somewhere* was her second, but I often develop out of sequence.) These rectangles of plastic, held together with tiny screws, changed my life. I still have the set. It smells like the red vinyl beanbag I smelted into on elementary school library tours. Thirteen years later, I am still learning – but trying my finger at teaching too.

Being disguised as a poor thinker makes people curious about how I process. "Can you read?" is a common question. I am not offended – okay, maybe a little – but here is the deal.

I read well, one word at a time, if the font size is at least 18. However, I prefer to take a mental picture of the page and file it, so that I may consider it and recall it at my leisure. The most efficient way for me to take in written information is to hear it. When I listen to audiobooks, my prized Great Teaching Courses, podcasts about history (*Hardcore History* by Dan Carlin is my favorite) or someone reading aloud to me, I go into my half-shell. I pull my shirt over my head, or if I'm feeling unusually puritanical, I lower my head into my hands or a lap pillow so that my vision will process only internal stimuli. I would simply close my eyes, but they do not reliably stay shut, as "simply" is as uncommon in my design as fatal bowling injuries. I use all my energy to process heard words into visual representations, and file accordingly. If I have to read the words first, it requires a double translation from the twenty-six visual symbols to word chunks, and then again to visual scenes of meaning.

Once you understand how you think best, I recommend taking charge of your own enrichment. My dalliance with education ended way before my stated mandated release at age twenty-one. I was at school, but rarely in it. Sometimes what is expected is not what is needed. Sometimes it's best to go with your flow.

Freeing yourself to be yourself takes practice, and not everyone will get you. Not everyone is supposed to get you – this is part of the axiom of authenticity. For example, my boyfriend, Jerry, asked me how my latest personal attendant (PA) interview went. My severe autism means twenty-four/seven care, so from time to time I have to hire new PAs. I can't talk, so to get the character scoop quickly, I always do a home-and-public practice run after they clear the non-axe-murder background check. This time, it did not go well. I know the "Oh, being 'friends' with her is going to be way too much trouble" look a mile away, and this was up close and not so personal. I was a little surprised, because this gal knew the deal. She loved my book and enthusiastically spoke about seeing me present to an auditorium full of teachers in training. Intellectually, the candidate knows I am bright but that I still have a host of unbecoming behaviors, which I blame on autism. I have a doctor's note for that. I am not proud of my remaining gross proclivities, but I am working on them – one nasty habit at a time. Progress for me is always slow. But this autistic tortoise plans to do well in this human race.

That weekend I was very stressed, as I was using most of my energy to make a writing deadline, so I struggled more than usual with impulse control. When I picked my skin bloody, dug at my privates and sniffed my crotch-ripe hand, and touched another's restaurant food, I could tell that her fledgling self-esteem was not sturdy enough to help me reliably navigate the world. She was profoundly embarrassed by what she called "my public masturbation." Now, at age forty-two, I am still unable to speak, but masturbation was checked off my IEP years ago – and what she witnessed ain't it. Please see the "Autistic Sex: For a Terrible Time, Call" chapter in my last book for more details. Later, she emailed plausible excuses why she could no longer consider the position, and went on her way, no worse for the autistic wear – but not better, either.

When will I be enough?

When will you be enough, fatty? Nice shoes, lesbo. (Please insert your relevant insult here.)

None of us are enough until we say we are.

Thankfully, I have a thick shell and patient gait. It is finally time to be enough and pick a different fight.

I just saw a hilarious clip by Lewis Black who pegged Sesame Street's Count von Count as an "**autistic vampire**." LOL. We do love our patterns. If that feisty old Jew, Lewis Black, can be non-PC about autism, so can we – because, for one thing, true funny is good for all that ails ya, and, two, there is power in humor – healing power, and lots of it.

Let's beat autism to the punch line. Each twisted autistic joke weakens its pity choke.

Let's take the gloves off – and you know where my hands have been. I'll throw the first aspie blow. I plan to take some of the hurt out of the autistic pain one sick lick at a time.

Changing perspective is what is needed. Autism is my prism, not my prison, so I plan to use my thick lens to perceive more funny. I have done it before.

My Smiling Shrink (SS) once helped me rid myself of a cadre of mental demons by making them seem cartoonish and small, becoming not powerful but ridiculous. We accomplished this with cognitive therapy in about two weeks. Every session, SS would take a few minutes to have me describe vividly the progressive demise of each lil' devil. It was empowering. I often laughed aloud, recalling Bill Cosby's line "I brought you into this world, I can take you out." (I later learned Cosby was referring to his dating style. But you get my point.) Changing perspective changes reality.

Dr. Temple Grandin wrote in *Unwritten Rules of Social Relationships: Decoding Social Mysteries through the Unique*

Perspectives of Autism. "Romantic relationships have a level of social complexity that I still don't understand today, and I consciously choose not to participate in them." Dr. Grandin chose to move past society's expectations and make her fulfilling relationships revolve around her work interests. Her life is satisfying and astoundingly productive. I, too, have decided I am enough.

Self-acceptance is really about freeing oneself from the perception of exclusion.

Exclusion is in the eye of the beholder.

Behold: My eyes choose to see more laughter on the bright horizon.

Huffington Post writer Todd Drenzer wrote, "If race, gender, sexual orientation, religion and obesity are all acceptable topics for humor, there's no reason that autism and disabilities in general should be exempt."

Moreover, "Humor is one of our most human qualities, and autistic people should be the subjects of it (and they should get to tell some of the jokes, too).

How do you want to make people feel? I want to make myself and others feel tickled to be more than enough. Let's make neurodiversity humor as common as juice stains in minivans.

I invite you to lighten up and join me. Enough B

Practical Implications:

1. Schedule time to be creative. We auts love structure. I plop down from nine to noon almost every day to type. I slow-poke letters productively, because I prepare mentally the night before. Autism shows me many wonderful perceptions, but she is a jealous love and requires my full energy and attention for that slow show. Typing takes a GREAT deal of effort. It is no time for creative thinking… I do that beforehand from the safety of my autistic shell. Smother (aka my Mother, Barbara Rentenbach) used to relentlessly pester me to schedule more activities. Now that she sees the fruits of my "chill time"

thinking, I am finally allowed to clock in and out of my autistic shell on a beautifully slow schedule.

2. Lighten up. "Never suppose that the humorous is the enemy of the serious. Lightness is a gift of the beginning – try to keep it with you for the whole stretch." Okay, that was Dr. Andrew Solomon, but when typing takes so long, quoting the prolifically smart seems prudent.

3. Prescient warning to neurotypicals seeking employment from us: Being "embarrassed of us" helps no one, and won't get you hired.

4. "The worst mistake anyone can make is to perceive anyone as lesser." Cowabunga dude – that was Andrew Solomon again. I might as well throw in another while I'm at it. In the same *New York Times* article, young Andrew got this wisdom from an older, accomplished writer: "Have a vision and cleave to it." Cleaving is hard but requisite, so keep pizza handy to fuel your turtle power.

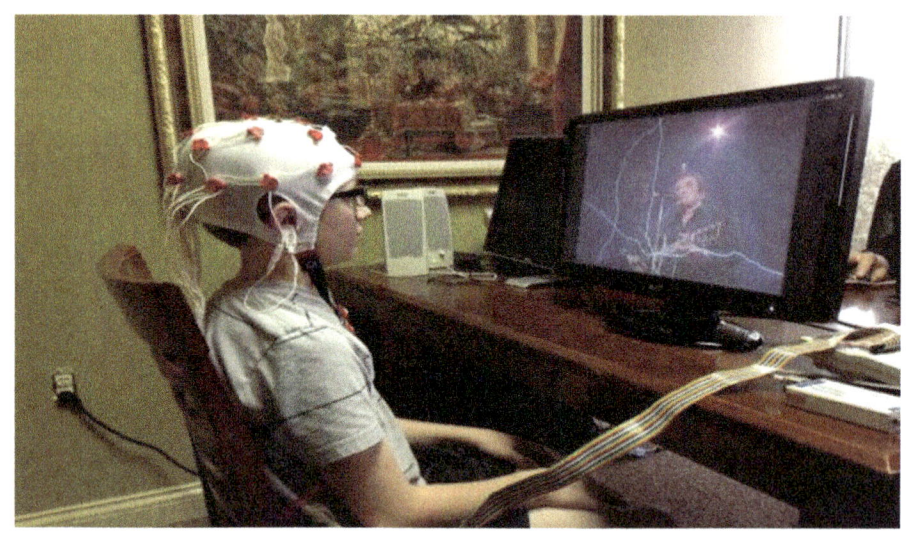

Told you A.B. was adorable.

Chapter 8

Anxiety Do's

by Lois Prislovksy

"When you understand the interplay between the brain and the mind, you are in a perfect position to understand the secret to overcoming fear, anxiety, and worry." Dr. Paul Jenkins

Anxiety is the most common and the most effectively treated psychological condition. I find practitioners like Dr. Paul Jenkins, Dr. Lissa Rankin, Dr. Mona Lisa Schulz, and Dr. Robert Leahy to be spot on with their shared sentiment that the cause and cure for anxiety are the brain and mind respectively. Once clients learn the role of their brain (an organ in their body) and their mind (thoughts which are in their control), they have the tools to manage anxiety.

The brain automatically responds to threat. The limbic system can't discern if danger is physically real. Despite orthodontic differences, a saber-toothed tiger and the cruelest popular girl in school heading your way may elicit the same physiological response. In *The Fear Cure*, Rankin classifies these as "True" and "False" fears. True fear is triggered when life and limb are threatened, and False fear is in your "imagination." Both types of fear are bad for your health if sustained, as our bodies are not designed to be frightened often. Chronic reaction to stress is toxic if unrelenting. The good news is that both True and False fears can be beneficial, if you learn how to filter the messages.

Below are five Do's to better manage thoughts, emotions, and health. The Don'ts will be in my next chapter. I am not afraid to tell you I did not have the attention span to put all ten tips in this one chapter. I tailored these as parenting tips for children. However, like juice boxes and popsicles, they are safe for self-care too.

To demonstrate each technique, I share how A.B. used each strategy to reduce his fears. A.B. was a twelve-year-old male client who literally presented with all six of the recognized anxiety disorders:

1. Specific Phobias
2. Panic Disorder
3. Obsessive-Compulsive Disorder (OCD)
4. Generalized Anxiety Disorder (GAD)
5. Social Anxiety Disorder (SAD) and
6. Post-Traumatic Stress Disorder (PTSD).

Do…

1. Facilitate Optimism. Teach your children the importance of perspective. In *Anxiety Free: Unravel your Fears Before They Unravel You,* Robert Leahy reminds us to "alter your perspective so that you are no longer a victim of your own mind. There's one great guiding principle: your fear level is determined not by the situation you find yourself in, but by your interpretation of that situation. When the interpretation changes, your whole sense of what is fearful and what is not changes with it."

   Adorable A.B. was open to learning and changing. And, yes, it helps to adore your clients. In fact, for me this draw is so crucial to being precisely who that client needs me to be every time, I honestly refer the potential client to another practitioner when that is missing. Before sending hate emails to my incompletely evolved self, please know that in twenty years of practice, I have referred away "hard to love" clients maybe five times. (Donald Sterling and Octomom types, I wish you all the best.)

   A pessimist can learn to be an optimist. Carol Dweck in *Mindset: The New Psychology of Success – How We Can Learn to Fulfill Our Potential* writes that, while temperament plays a role, people can be taught "the growth mindset." Those who learn to process as optimists are more likely to take action in response to stressors, whereas pessimists may feel defeated, making them less likely to take constructive actions. Cognitive Behavior Therapy (CBT), a form of talk therapy that emphasizes the role of thinking about how we feel and what we do, is a robust approach to making the mindset change when you are ready to reduce the pain of anxiety.

Rational Emotive Therapy (RET) is another empirically sound approach to examining one's thoughts – and challenging the message of fear – by questioning its truth using logic and experience. Albert Ellis presents this application well in his book, *How to Control Your Anxiety Before It Controls You.*

A.B. was intellectually bright, and had splinter gifts in vocabulary and analytical skills, so we started with both CBT and RET. I explained both theories to A.B., and we used the terms associated with each as we worked. I find that transparency is empowering and effective. I should also note that our practice is set up as one-stop shopping for psychoeducational needs, so I rarely work with a client without the benefit of having a full psychoeducational report. This key information allows us to design strategies that build on each client's individual strengths.

When A.B. first came to me, he struggled with anxiety so much that he was unable to go to school. His father changed his entire work schedule and began to homeschool him. Father and son were clearly close and affectionate. A.B.'s father was a strong positive force in his life. A.B. presented as socially less mature than his peers, so I saw Dad and A.B. together at every session. This collaboration proved productive, as we all learned together, and his father was quick to reinforce in other settings what was practiced in session.

A.B. used CBT and RET to help identify and deconstruct each of his troubling thoughts and behaviors. A.B.'s analytical strengths and hyper-verbal presentation allowed him to navigate these quickly. He also had a well-deserved ADHD label and rarely sat still long enough for such introspection and discussion, but we made it easier by encouraging A.B. to be physically active when contemplating. Like many individuals with ADHD Combined type, he thinks best when moving. (I resemble that remark. In fact, I'm typing this while pedaling a bike – don't worry, it's a stationary bike – I learned that lesson.) In my office, A.B. frequented a large Pilates ball, a mini-trampoline, a couch, and a spinning office chair. I often playfully reinforced his breakthrough ideas with a "nitrous boost" spin of his chair. Sometimes you don't need a child psychologist, just a child-like psychologist. (In developmental biology, neoteny refers to retaining childlike qualities into later development.) A.B. needed encouragement to lighten up and use his childhood powers of curiosity, playfulness, creativity, and flexibility to help him break through fears.

With shaping, fun and respectful peer-like dialogue, A.B. was able to stay on task and generate his own solutions. In weekly sessions with homework, A.B. cognitively worked through almost one anxiety roadblock per week.

2. Practice Mindfulness. Mindfulness is an excellent way to process anxiety. It changes emotional reactions, which are often unconscious, into a chosen, controlled, fully conscious response. With mindfulness, one can choose to only get angry on purpose, and other fun tricks. Suppressing emotions is proven to decrease well-being. Specifically, holding anger and fear is counterproductive to health. Mindfulness allows one to feel and validate emotions and then move on, Sylvia Boorstein, in her book *It's Easier Than You Think*, makes a case that pain is inevitable, but suffering is optional. The key is to own the emotion, and then do with it as you will. Rankin's *The Fear Cure* recommends examining "false" fears long enough to let them teach you "wake up" messages: "Fear points a bony finger at everything that needs to be healed in our lives, and if we're brave enough to heal it, courage blossoms and peace is the prize."

Phobias are reactions that get stuck in a feedback loop. These conditioned fears can be extinguished by increasing awareness, and restoring control to the user of the brain. I often use hypnosis as a fast way to help clients increase mindfulness. This may sound paradoxical, as hypnotherapy focuses on unconscious knowing. I find it most effective when used in combination with self-awareness learning. I start by explaining the approach, and the logic behind it – even down to the specific words I may be using – as we Ericksonian hypnotherapists are trained to use connotations that have more value to that particular client.

A.B. enjoyed learning about hypnosis and being hypnotized. I am confident about this, because after each hypnosis exercise, I ask the client to fill out a brief feedback form with a satisfaction rating. (A.B. was not one to tell me what he thinks I want to hear. His Prefrontal Cortex was not there yet.) He answered questions like, "The most difficult part of this exercise was <u>preparing for it.</u>" "The most helpful part of this session was <u>I don't feel as scared of bees.</u>" "I am not yet ready to <u>hang out in a bee hive.</u>" And "I am just now starting to realize <u>bees are nothing to me.</u>" As I do with all clients, we recorded the actual hypnosis so he could take home the CD and practice it four to five more times before our next visit. This is advantageous for many reasons. For one, the subject can hear that the content is positive and can safely take full ownership of his/her transformation. Second, hypnosis is in essence a state of extreme focus, and practicing sustained attention is beneficial, especially to those with ADHD. Third, all hypnosis is self-hypnosis; as A.B. practiced with the CD at home, he became better at self-regulation.

To keep A.B. interested in continuing specific neural growth and integration, we talked about people who, like him, practiced purposeful thinking and were able to enter higher phases of functioning. For instance, in *Super Brain: Unleashing the Explosive Power of Your Mind to Maximize Health, Happiness, and Spiritual Well-Being*, Deepak Chopra and Rudolph Tanzi share accounts of Tibetan Buddhist monks who use this same feedback loop, combined with meditation techniques, to warm their entire bodies by focusing on getting warmer. When they maintain focus on this intention, they can sit in ice caves, meditating overnight, while wearing nothing more than thin, silk saffron robes.

Saffron was not A.B.'s color, yet he was able to achieve similar brain/body connection in his own hyper-focused, relaxed state of hypnosis. For example, in addition to considering practical problem-solving suggestions during hypnosis, A.B. was able to:

1) Numb his hand to almost 100%
2) Hold and feel an imaginary tennis racket
3) Auditorily follow a nonexistent fly and
4) Describe a flower he was able to "see" on the floor in front of him.

A.B. gained confidence. His brain was beginning to follow orders from his mind reliably.

With continued CBT, RET and hypnotherapy, A.B. was able to conquer about one phobia per week: crowds/loud noises, bees, tests, and "brick and mortar" schools. With those fears better managed, he was able to participate in neurofeedback training for more gains.

3. Consider Neurofeedback (NFB). Research and technology have advanced to allow neurotherapists to target specific areas of the brain responsible for an individual's anxiety. Plus, it's crazy fun to play video games with your mind. Look, Ma, no hands! Seriously, that is what neurofeedback treatment for ADHD and anxiety involves at Psychoeducational Network. I did it myself. It helped. (But it is not all fun and games – neurofeedback clients are required to refrain from alcohol on the evenings prior to training. A.B. seemed okay with it, but I tried to get another opinion – then finally, the third guy I asked, who was ringing up my Heineken at the gas station, said it was fine with him.) It is a non-invasive technique proven to be safe and effective. Using an electroencephalograph to monitor brain waves, and a system of positive reinforcement, clients learn how to train their brains to regulate anxiety. For more information about neurofeedback, please check out Dr. Rex Cannon's videos at www.psychoeducationalnetwork.com.

A.B.'s success with NFB was featured in a HealthlineNews article by Penny Williams, "Can Neurofeedback help kids with ADHD press the restart button?" Below is an excerpt from that article. Please note that it is primarily about A.B.'s ADHD, but his co-morbid anxiety also improved.

A.B.'s Mom, "After the second or third week, my son noted that his thoughts were 'quieter than normal,' which he really liked. Overall, after a month of neurofeedback, we noticed reduced anxiety and better responses to our requests to do things he didn't like, such as homework and chores. We were happy with the differences we saw in his behavior."

4. Encourage Generosity. To help others break the cycle of anxiety ruminations, share – When in doubt, think out.

The Dalai Lama states, "Helping others does not mean we do this at our own expense. Wise people want happiness. How to do this? By cultivating compassion, by cultivating altruism. When they care for others, they themselves are the first to benefit – they are the first to get maximum happiness. That's real wisdom."

In conjunction with CBT, RET, hypnosis, and NFB, we encouraged A.B. to begin giving to others. By this time, A.B. had transitioned back to a "brick and mortar" school. He had many opportunities to give. I asked A.B., "What could you do, say, or give to help your Dad, Mom, sister, or someone at school?" This outward thinking eased A.B. into becoming less egocentric and immature, and more likeable – all of which reduced his social anxiety and his OCD thought loops. He often chose to give compliments to a girl in his class whom he perceived as struggling with low self-esteem. By opening his heart and mind to others, A.B. began to break his self-absorption patterns and feelings of being frightened and alone.

5. Listen. It is both comforting and cathartic to be heard. In *The Whole-Brain Child: Revolutionary Strategies to Nurture Your Child's Developing Mind*, renowned neuropsychiatrist Dr. Daniel Siegel shares compelling information about brain anatomy and how to foster secure attachment by listening to your child with these four S's in mind: Seen, Safe, Soothed, and Secure. Parents are encouraged to see the inner-life needs of the child, provide safety with comfort and compassion, and soothe by reaching out to connect when children are distressed. Secure children are then

resilient and able to deal with life's challenges with flexibility and strength. A.B. was able to process his PTSD with this type of support.

Let your child talk freely and honestly about his/her feelings when he/she is ready. At this time, do not try to fix; just listen with openness and understanding. In *Living Buddha, Living Christ,* Thich Nhat Hanh explains the Buddhist term *vipasyana* (looking deeply) as observing something or someone with so much concentration that the distinction between observer and observed disappears. When we are able to let go of barriers between ourselves and others, understanding is possible. **Once isolation is gone, fear is diminished, and growth is imminent.**

A.B. also had a bad habit of interrupting and talking over others. By mirroring our active listening and role-playing, A.B. improved his listening skills and decreased his panic attacks.

Remember that anxiety is not always a bad state of being. It means you are thinking about risks and opportunities; however, when fear immobilizes goal progression, it's time to do something different. In *Brainstorm: The Power and Purpose of the Teenage Brain,* Siegel reminds us, "our brains are programmable and we are the programmers."

Godsends: Mike and Barbara Rentenbach
aka DD (Dearest Dad) and Smother.

Chapter 9
I of the Storm
by Barb Rentenbach

"Anxiety is the handmaiden of Creativity." T. S. Eliot

Lately, my anxiety and obsessive compulsions are hurricane force. Previously, I would just board up the windows, get under covers, and await sunrise. Not this time. I earned this power and I am taking it. I plan to funnel my energy and create one path at a time. Today and yesterday, I allowed my worries and repetitive thoughts to whirl only around this writing. Lets hear it for FEMA (Funneling Energy Muse Approach)

Storm watchers may be interested to know the generating factors. Here is my Hurricane Barb conversation with SS:

L = Barb, I see you are struggling with biting your arm frequently and breaking your glasses.

Me = Impressive. Did they teach you that in school, or did you catch glimpses of my gnawed wrist? Or perhaps the excitement of you darting around the room to avoid my grabbing lunges finally registered?

L = All of the above. Do you want to talk about it?

Me = Desperately, but typing may have to do. I'll save the biggie storm surge for last. But here are few things that picked up wind:

My beloved house manager recently quit smoking. This is a good thing, I know, but not without blows of irritation. Plus, my parents scheduled a "home inspection" this week. Which is the official business term for when my parents snoop all through my home every few months. I rather enjoy the open house and extra attention to detail.

But the exercise does raise the staff's stress considerably. Which means we all feel it. My house manager made sure all was in order and passed with flying colors… except for a little bathroom issue which is all on me. Here is an except from Inspector Smother's report:

"Secondly, about your bath time, I was appalled to know that you slosh the water around so much that you have damaged the tiles on the floor with all the water… the PAs apparently let you play like crazy and slide back and forth, pour water over your head, etc… and much water goes out of the tub… when did you start all that? I am going to write a letter to all the PAs about NOT letting you do all those shenanigans… not flooding the bathroom with water… please stop that before we have to put a new floor in… and why do you do that anyway? I will ask them to just get you out if that continues… you can splash around in a pool. The house looks beautiful. And you are very fortunate to have (name redacted for privacy) taking such good care of it and she says you help too!! Now let's get these things addressed please...

L = So, what do you plan to do about "bath time shenanigans"?

Me = I see a bigger tub in my future.

Now, back to my weather forecast.
My muse work is really picking up. I am not used to so many people counting on me.

L = You are taking on a great deal. Finishing your book this month is a daunting project – 60,000 words is a lot for anyone. And planning two big-time LOUD MUTE RADIO shows featuring Donna Williams and then Dr. Temple Grandin is international high-performance stuff.

Me = Donna Williams and Temple Grandin are my heroes. Work is a godsend, and that's as it should be. I have always been good at being; I need to get better at doing.

If that were the all of it, we would be looking at a topical depression – but there is more.

A few weeks ago, Smother told me my insurance would soon no longer pay for my antidepressant/anxiety medicine. Raised frugal, stoic, and feeling more happy and clear-headed than I have ever been, I thought – now is the time to just say no to Lexapro. Sorry, Nancy Reagan, it often takes me years to process slogans.

L = Yes, I remember you told me you were going to quit Lexapro cold turkey.

Me = Well, I've never been a fan of turkey, and cold recipes bite. So I tapered off.

L = But, you still had bad withdrawal symptoms?

Me = Bingo. Remember that "no Barb" Sunday morning?

L = Yes. You did not show up to work with me. I went over to check on you and you were still in bed and typed "I'm sad but will trudge through and leave bread crumbs for others to find their way easier – plus I don't need the carbs."

Me = Right, that Sunday morning I did not officially wake up because I did not sleep. I was in a sticky smog-jam of confusion and sleepy restlessness. Autistic fires burn faster and hotter and the smoke stings and occludes like fear gas. This was different.

You know how I love my morning bowls of Cheerios? No more. I lost the attraction, and several pounds, already. I gained fifteen pounds when I started taking Lexapro years ago. Serotonin must be heavy.

And remember when I got back to work I told you, "Lexapro has done something with my personhood. It sucked the life out of me like a Kennedy Chappaquiddick drive. It is time to cut my seatbelt and break the window. I'll free myself and tell the world how."

L = I do – so do you think you are ready to share?

Me = Well, I can't take credit for musing a solution about the sleeplessness or irritability. Sleeping just got better passively in a few days. As for irritability… recommending biting and breaking eyeglasses seems ill advised.

Below is breadcrumb debris that may be worth salvage.

Practical Implications:

1. Hypnosis helped. I asked SS to hypnotize me before this writing. I was overwhelmed, and needed to calmly focus my attention on clarity and patience. Normally patience is my virtue. But I got swooped up in my perfect storm. Time to reset.

    I process best when I isolate my senses. SS loaned me a hoodie so I could better focus during hypnosis. When I listen intently, I go into my half-shell. If no petite, bull-dyke hoodie is available, I pull my shirt over my head, or if I'm feeling unusually puritanical, I lower my head into my hands or a lap pillow so my vision will process only internal stimuli. I would close my eyes but they do not reliably stay shut. I use all my energy to process heard words into visual representations, and file accordingly.

2. Embrace eye floaters as pets. For me, eye floaters were an unexpected but not unwelcome Lexapro-withdrawal side effect.

    I adopted a previously concealed translucent sea horse named Calypso, and I now visit much more frequently with my old friend "Go Go," a thick, folded floater worm with a fluorescent green stripe.

3. Focus on one thought at a time.

    This helped me manage my anxiety overload better than anything else.

I start every workday with SS touching one finger to my back to push my apraxia "manual-override button" so I can solo type what I want to do, and in what order. I usually type a paragraph or two to get started. Then, as I accomplish, SS flits here and there, talking about related but additional tasks scampering across her nat brain. I need to work differently now. I explained it in redneck terms I knew SS would understand: "Stop the shotgun-info blasts, and laser focus with me." She did. Then, I typed only one small thing. I did it and only it. And then I typed the next thing.

Med MD tells me, "Some people feel normal within a few months of quitting the drug." Stay tuned for upcoming miracles.

Love more organic B

Look ma, no saffron robe.

Chapter 10
Anxiety Don'ts
by Lois Prislovsky

"The will to win is important, but the will to prepare is vital." Joe Paterno (Our editor thinks I should take this out. But, I figure we can learn something from everybody, and quoting only perfect people is limiting. This chapter is about preparing for anxiety.)

To recap: anxiety is not innately bad and can liberate us to be and do more.

It is amazing how quickly the brain complies with what the mind is asking it to do.

Yesterday afternoon, I took Eli and a couple of friends to Jump Jam. I am happy to give an enthusiastic plug for our local trampoline park. We have been to many, but Jump Jam is our favorite as it has few rules and dozens of activities. I evangelize often that people should move more, and what is more joyous than jumping? Dodge ball while jumping, that's what! The owner appreciates my old-lady diversity addition and gives me free passes for Psychoeducational Network practitioners to give to our clients. Beats smiley face stickers.

One of the more challenging games at Jump Jam is a two-inch-wide flex line, stretched out twenty feet and suspended about three feet above a foam pit. The idea is to tightrope across. It seems impossible, yet I can do it all the way there and back. Ice-cave-sitting monks have no monopoly on doing weird, interesting stuff. Now, being five foot tall and bowlegged helps, but anyone can do it. It just takes practicing: letting go, focusing on your destination, and taking one step at time.

When working with clients, we are not performing research, where it is important to isolate variables. The intention with a client is to facilitate goal attainment as efficiently as possible, so we often use multiple techniques simultaneously.

For examples in this follow-up anxiety chapter, I will discuss another bright young man with Anxiety and ADHD diagnoses who quickly became successful at preparing for and managing his fear-based difficulties.

C.D. was five years young, and came to us for oppositional defiance issues related to anxiety. C.D. had refusal meltdowns at school, the dinner table, and doctor's visits. *"I can't do it!"* was his mantra. In *The Explosive Child: A New Approach for Understanding and Parenting Easily Frustrated, Chronically Inflexible Children*, Ross Green says it so well: "Behaviorally challenging kids are challenging because they're lacking the skills not to be challenging." Furthermore, in *I Might Be You: An Exploration of Autism and Connection,* Barb taught us the truth about consequences so often being ineffective with fear-related behaviors – plus the critical component of presuming competence. With this "people do better when they know better" foundation, C.D. quickly learned to better manage his thoughts and behaviors.

Presented with his parents' permission, below are C.D.'s session notes (emailed to the client 24 hours after each meeting to recap and reinforce), which may help illuminate his progressive steps.

7-16-2014 = First session went well. C.D. and I were able to build rapport quickly. His mom observed and participated in the full session. We began with a few confidence-building exercises to help C.D. understand some of his considerable strengths. He catches on very quickly and was able to work second-grade multiplication exercises involving zeros. C.D. enjoyed this and grasped the structure and pattern easily. We even discussed his intellectual strengths as compared to others on a bell-shaped curve. C.D. thinks best when moving, so we did a few fast-paced letter-reading and catching games while he was on a mini-trampoline to improve his processing speed. It is important to keep this processing-speed work fun, to have C.D. associate it positively, and to reduce performance-related anxiety. He was beautifully cooperative and open to talking about some fears, social situations, and hand flapping. We began introducing body-language exercises to help him regulate his anxiety. The plan is to use a multimodal approach involving the computer, role-playing games, and mind/body control techniques to help C.D. with self-regulation, anxiety, attention, frustration tolerance, and processing speed. Only minor adjustments to C.D.'s diet are recommended as his parents have done an outstanding job with that. His screen time and home activity levels also seem to be healthful. Exercise is the best treatment for ADHD and Anxiety, so we discussed increasing team activities like soccer. Mom is open to coaching C.D. in AYSO soccer to facilitate more social opportunities in a safe, positive environment. I emailed Mom, and the AYSO regional director, to begin the process. C.D. is eager to learn. We will incorporate some challenging activities soon, to help him practice breaking through the hard stuff and losing the "I can't do it" mentality. = 1 session

7-21-2014 = Mom, C.D., and I worked together the entire session. C.D. was very focused and cooperative. We began with a visual-memory exercise to help C.D. remember words, and eventually entire paragraphs and pages, using detailed and novel visual-memory techniques. We also did a "flinching game" activity to help C.D. with mind/body control and improve processing speed. He seemed to enjoy all our exercises today. C.D. showed remarkable attention to detail on a "memory for faces" computer game, designed to help him to improve social skills. We did many above-grade-level math problems and mazes, to encourage working through difficult times, but he found those not challenging enough to be difficulties. Instead, we worked on him being more mindful of saying, "I can't do it" by positively reinforcing "I can do it" activities with an enthusiastic chair spin. Action-oriented positive reinforcement works well with C.D. We also discussed and practiced the use of a large ball to help him stimulate his core muscles enough to remain conversational and appropriate at the dinner table. Mom and I made a plan for her to email me any current struggles prior to each session, so that we may plan specific coping strategies. We also talked about how this strong-minded young man does well with the Socratic method, where we don't correct him but instead ask C.D. questions so he can find his own answers. Excellent progress. Soon we will work on his doctor anxieties, and I also look forward to doing some role-playing exercises with C.D. next week to help him deal with a long school day next Wednesday. = 1 session

7-28-2014 = Today, we focused on helping C.D. with his fear of doctors. Just as Mom reported, C.D. has developed considerable denial over the situation. By the end of the session, we were able to finally break through that, and C.D. began using the language that his shot and doctor's visit are going to happen. We empowered him by letting him play with the contents of a pediatric medical bag and wear the white lab coat. C.D. was open to this and role-played some while he processed what was going to happen on Wednesday. He also cooperated fairly well with me, doing a brief guided relaxation "with his Mom." The idea was to introduce C.D. to hypnosis by listening with his Mom, and being calm, as she did a short hypnosis exercise designed to help him be able to mentally experience an enjoyable bowling time whenever he wished to feel happier and in control. We also reviewed some pictures of other children his age who got shots, to show that it is a reality. Next, we helped C.D. prepare a three-point request letter to give to the doctor who will be giving him his shot on Wednesday: "To the doctor who will give me my shot. 1. I want you to slow down. 2. I want you to be nice to me, C.D., 3. I want to play monster truck game on my iPad immediately after getting my shot." Mom also agrees to take him bowling after he does the doctor's visit well. She also understands the importance of keeping her expectations positive and rewarding him ASAP. I think CD is ready to be successful at the doctor's. I look forward to hearing how it goes. = 1 session

A week later, C.D.'s Mom emailed me the great news: "Checkup went the best it ever has. He sat still for the shot, expressed his anxiety and did not defer or deny, and we went bowling afterward. Success!" She also reported he is loving soccer and is thriving at school.

The following Anxiety Don'ts further breakdown proactive steps in anxiety management.

Don't:

1. Don't overprotect. You are a model for your child, regarding how to handle stress, fears, and problems. Renowned thinker and science-fiction writer Robert A. Heinlein wrote, "Don't handicap your children by making their lives too easy." In Norman Doidge's book, *The Brain That Changes Itself*, we are reminded that

scientists know that physical exercise prolongs the life of extant neurons, while exposure to new experiences, environments, and challenging thinking promotes neurogeneration of new glial cells. With experience and practice, these neural pathways establish tracks, and then quicken, just like a sled going down a snowy hill. **Parents who assist their children with anxiety in gaining exposure to novel environments, and working through problem solving as independently as possible, promote brain growth and development.**

C.D.'s parents wisely prepared him with the tools to discover his own solutions BEFORE meltdowns. When C.D. felt seen, safe, soothed, and secure, he worked with his Mom and me on collaborative and proactive problem-solving approaches. In Ross Green's *The Explosive Child,* he describes this model as "Plan B," consisting of three steps: Empathy, Define the Problem, and Invitation. "The Empathy Step involves gathering information from your child to understand his concern or perspective... The Define the Problem Step involves communicating your concern or perspective... The Invitation step is when you and your child discuss and agree on a solution that is realistic."

We also used the Socratic method to help C.D. know his thoughts. This old-timey philosopher – even old-timey-er than Bill Clinton, promoted Ask, Don't Tell. Don't just tell the child the solution; have the child think it through on their own while you give positive reinforcement and active listening support. This stimulates critical thinking, and such dialogue illuminates ideas because the learning is now multimodal. Multimodal learning (using as many senses as possible) is best for mastery and retention. We remember about 10% of what we read, 20% of what we hear, 80% of what we speak, and 90% of what we do. Having your child teach the information to you is a wonderful strategy, because when you implement what you have just learned, you instantly make mistakes. **Mistakes force the brain to focus and rethink alternatives**.

Children need to practice handling stress, fears, deadlines and mistakes. The acceptance of "not always getting it right" is a lesson we need to demonstrate and teach. It promotes brain growth and life-long learners.

Socrates Joke: Plato says to Socrates on their first meeting, "Why don't you ever have a girlfriend?" Socrates responds, "You ask too many questions."

Persevere and remember to laugh. Laughter is like cross-fit for the brain. It engages and strengthens multiple regions across the whole brain and promotes flexibility. Dr. Daniel Goleman, a brilliant psychologist who conducted vast research for his Emotional & Social Intelligence books, states: "Laughter helps people think more broadly and associate more freely."

2. Don't be too permissive. Letting children do whatever they want, whenever they want, does not "take the pressure off." In fact, too much freedom may cause a child anxiety. Children become fearful and overwhelmed when given too many choices and denied limit setting. Set boundaries. Provide structure and clear, consistent rules so your children may concentrate on learning, growing, and exercising self-control, leaving the responsibilities of mature decision-making to you.

C.D.'s Mom followed through on the structured agreement. After completing what he was expected to do, C.D. earned bowling fun as planned. Understanding that clinical trials show that regular exercise works just as well as – or better than – medication for anxiety, C.D.'s family also helped him increase his daily exercise, which again added structure and consistent rules.

"If you do what is easy, your life will be hard. If you do what is hard, your life will be easy." Les Brown

3. Don't forget to practice relaxation. It is physically impossible to be in a relaxed state and experience anxiety. The states are mutually exclusive. There are many self-regulation relaxation techniques you may teach your child. Research simple breathing and mindfulness exercises to see which may best fit your family's

needs. Then, practice those with your child several times during non-stressful, quality, one-on-one times. Later, when anxiety does arise, the child will be armed with more ability to self-regulate, with these now-familiar exercises that have been paired with happy, calm times.

Here are the exercises C.D. practiced with his Mom:

- Practice the following steps three times a day, for five days, for three to five minutes per session:

Step 1. Breathe on purpose – to increase blood flow to the thinker. (This reverses fight-or-flight-or-freeze blood flow.) Inhale through nose deeply.

Step 2. Hold a deep belly breath for ten seconds – SMILE and assume dominance posture.
Prior to learning this strategy, we taught C.D. about the power of body language and his power to program his brain.

Step 3. Blow out through mouth verbally or mentally saying, "release," "peace," "Batman"… or whatever word works for you.

If your child learns well through videos, I highly recommend these two TED talks:

- Amy Cuddy's "Your Body Language Shapes Who You Are" = http://bit.ly/1wRPBDC
- Kelly McGonigal's "How to Make Stress Your Friend" = http://bit.ly/1rF7KXp

Some of the concepts from the aforementioned videos we shared with C.D. were examples of how our physiology affects our feelings. CD knew that when people are happy, they smile; however, he also learned that when people put their mouth muscles into the shape of a smile (like when holding a pencil across their mouth) it also makes them feel happy. C.D. learned that feeling powerful also works both ways. Like Amy Cuddy suggests, C.D. practiced standing in a powerful Batman-like posture so he could make his brain release chemicals that would make him feel more safe, confident, and strong. Cuddy is a social psychologist who presented significant research showing how two minutes of such dominant body posture literally raises testosterone and lowers cortisol, your stress hormone.

C.D. also learned from psychologist Kelly McGonigal's content that if he thought about his worry as beneficial – it would be by giving him more oxygen to think and move.

C.D. was only five years old, so we just explained highlights, but McGonigal's research is fascinating. The Harvard study reported that those who re-envisioned their stress as energizing and helpful became less anxious. Additionally, "the physical stress response changed." McGonigal explains that, "in a typical stress response, your heart rate goes up, and your blood vessels constrict... And this is one of the reasons that chronic stress is sometimes associated with cardiovascular disease. It's not really healthy to be in this state all the time. But in the study, when participants viewed their stress response as helpful, their blood vessels stayed relaxed... Their heart was still pounding, but this is a much healthier cardiovascular profile. It actually looks a lot like what happens in moments of joy and courage.... And this is really what the new science of stress reveals, that how you think about stress matters."

4. Don't reinforce negative perceptions. Teach your children to **choose accountability over victim-hood.** As Victor Frankl writes in *Man's Search for Meaning*, "In the concentration camp, every circumstance conspires to make the prisoner lose his hold. All the familiar goals in life are snatched away. What alone remains is "the last of human freedoms – the ability to choose one's attitude in a given set of circumstances." Parents and children can do this. When roadblocks come up, we have the power to choose our response.

C.D.'s repetitive "I CAN'T do it!" phrase let him know he was feeling afraid to fail. By trying new, hard exercises with him where we all failed often, we modeled and reinforced the perspective that messing up is not a problem. In fact, failing really helps us get better, faster. C.D. learned he could respond to his fear of failure differently – he practiced trying and thus growing.

We encouraged C.D. to feel his fear, then be grateful for it, as **FEAR is needed for courage.**

C.D. learned that failures teach us how to be successful. He replaced his self-defeating maxim with, "I can try." (I was rooting for "I can do it!" but the growth choice was his.)

5. Don't give up. Avoidance is the primary way most of us deal with anxiety – which is not the best practice. In her book, *Mindset: The New Psychology of Success – How We Can Learn to Fulfill Our Potential*, Carol S. Dweck confirms how a "growth mindset" can change the meaning of failure, not by eliminating the distress and anxiety, but by taking control of the painful experience so that it does not define you but rather is processed as a problem to be faced and learned from for betterment." **When we take advantage of the opportunity to change and better ourselves, it takes the hurt out of the pain.**

Furthermore, Dweck writes, "People with the growth mindset know that it takes time for potential to flower," as she describes researching Paul Cezanne's early paintings – and finding they were pretty bad. It took time for Cezanne to become Cezanne. Give your child the time and permission to make mistakes and learn – while becoming his/her highest self.

Understanding the logic behind strategies is essential to help a child better manage fear. Be straightforward about what you are suggesting, and the reasons why it works. C.D. learned the whys, and he was inspired to do and be more.

Meaning matters. Meaning automatically improves motivation. Whenever possible, explain the "Why." A child with test anxiety may say, "Why do we take tests? It's so stupid. I know this stuff." A parent may explain that actually research shows test taking significantly improves learning and recall. The act of being tested requires the learner to reshape and categorize the information into personal, meaningful associations, which then become accessible, long-term memories.

Meaning matters. That is why placebos have an effect on the brain. The human brain anticipates outcomes, and that anticipation has a real effect. C.D. understood the reasons why his trying would improve his performance and decrease his fear. His choice to try made sense to C.D., so his positive outcome was a product of both practice and expectation.

The Worry Solution: Using Breakthrough Brain Science to Turn Stress and Anxiety into Confidence and Happiness, by Martin Rossman, expands on the positive side of worry. Rossman sees it as a way for us to turn over and solve a problem in our minds. Worry need not be a negative cycle. One can learn to "worry well" and "harness the very power of imagination that creates worry and stress... sort them into those you can and cannot do something about, and tap the wisdom buried deep within you to help solve problems creatively.... Not only can you start to see a change in your stress levels immediately, but with regular practice, you may literally alter the worry pathways in your brain – and 'hardwire' yourself for calmness and clarity."

You matter. Thoughts become chemical. Treat yourself well in advance.

At my home with boyfriend, Jerry, on my favorite Holiday. Word on the street is, "I GIVE OUT FULL SIZE CANDY BARS!" Guilty as charged with love generous giver and receiver Bee.

Chapter 11

Who Do You Think You Are?

by Barb Rentenbach

"Humanity needs exactly you." Me

Who do you think you are? Does it depend on who is asking and how? Is Johnny Carson inviting you to the chair beside him or is a George Zimmerman making deadly assumptions?

My Smiling Shrink lives next door and I visit often. SS is nearly devoid of taste and employs decorators to help the place not look like a P.E. teacher's closet. (This is no news flash to SS, so save your pity; she has adapted well to her disability.) One hired fancy gun instructed her to buy a pair of huge, gold-painted, broken chairs, covered in insanely textured pink fabric, which the decorator spied in a junk store. Turns out, after being stripped, repaired, and upholstered by a more sane craftsman, the chairs are recognized as true antique, museum-quality mahogany masterpieces worth more than anything else cheap SS owns. We call them the "Who do you think you are?" chairs and I plop my plumpness on them at every opportunity, because that I can do. I can choose to think I deserve to sit at the head of the table.

Philosopher King Marcus Aurelius wrote, "The universe is change; our life is what our thoughts make it."

As we consider the complexities and power of perspective, please allow me to give what I have to offer – my perspective, which is much safer to ship than Winston Churchill's proposal, "I have nothing to offer but blood, toil, tears, and sweat. "

My hard-earned perspective may be best packaged in my last audiobook, and as an Amazon review says, (5.0 out of 5 stars if I do re-type so myself), I hope, **"You'll laugh, you'll cry but most importantly you'll look at the world differently!"**

I sent five free audiobooks to outstanding bloggers who help spread the message of hope.

For those bloggers who choose to participate, their readers simply clicked a link, and vi-ola – complimentary audiobook. It was an early autistic bird special, as only the first five entries from each blog got the bookworm.

What does a giveaway have to do with perspective? Everything. Life is perspective – and life stinks without giving. (Receiving does not suck either, so let's keep this going.)

What inspired me to do this giveaway was the recent controversy concerning the autism chapter in Andrew Solomon's artfully researched bestseller, *Far From the Tree*. (The book took him ten years to write. I can relate to that type of perseverance, even though I suspect Andrew may type with all ten well-manicured fingers, and not just one autistically wired, nail-bitten digit like me, but who am I to judge if he needs extra time.) Many in our autistic community wish to boycott his book, as they find it to be filled with harmful parenting horror stories. I wrote on that below, and have since heard the chapter. We non-verbal auts often enjoy learning with audiobooks, as we can usually do so under our own steam; which is why this giveaway was audiobook specific.

Solomon is a master storyteller. He relays tales of parents in harrowing, sustained pain. He gifts these real people a voice. These overwhelmed parents were heard. I often write of the healing power of being heard.

Below is my comment following Jessica Wilson's "Diary of a Mom" account of this controversy. The next comment comes from a special-education counselor (the kind of "special" nobody, I mean NOBODY wants to be). See Dick run about his trouble with hardness.

barb typed:
it is true autism is hard. i have autism, the hard kind. but i have decided to be up to the challenge, as my parents did, because there is no other palatable option. andrew solomon is no enemy of those of us who are here with jess to "demystify the condition and to humanize the people behind the label in the public eye" because andrew is genuinely trying to know. so should we. andrew will learn from us and we from him. life is perspective. to live a balanced, wholehearted life

we are wise to learn how we are perceived so we may better connect with others and each respect who we chose to be. so, i just purchased "far from the tree" to learn more of those perspectives, knowing they may be hard to hear. i hope andrew will repay my respect and purchase my audiobook, "i might be you: an exploration of autism and connection" so he may learn my hard truths. may we all transform "years of accumulated slights" to the now of empathy and compassion. sometimes hard to hear but listening b

Dick says: July 12, 2013 at 10:22 pm *I'm skeptical that anyone can honestly write "i have autism, the hard kind." I am a 50 y.o. rehabilitation counselor and I work with adults and kids with autism – the hard kind – every day. None can read. None can write. None even know what autism is. THAT is "the hard kind." I also work with adults and kids that have autism – the not so hard kind – who read and write and drive. But people who have "the hard kind" of autism can't write about it. They can't even talk about it.*

Barb says: July 15, 2013 at 10:50 am *dear dick, it is my hope you will be open to knowing that many of us who are disguised as poor thinkers are in fact more like you than you may choose to believe. we may have a variety of physical and mental challenges confounded by profound difficulties with communication which shroud our humanity. i invite you to please take a few moments to read this link about how some of us with the hard kind have broken through with lots of hard work and sustained focus. thank you for caring. real b "a note on how this book was written" http://muleandmuseproductions.com/about-the-book-i-might-be-you/*

I wrote the measured response to Dick above because I am learning we all do better when we know better. From my hard front row seat to autism, rehabilitation counseling, and special education, I learned that believing one's students are mentally deficient and not capable of sentient thought – much less writing – leads to not teaching Dick. (Oh, did I leave out a comma? If only I could learn to write…)

Almost 100 percent of my teachers thought that way and treated me accordingly – as a lesser being. It only took one teacher who taught from her heart to my heart to change my reality and course. Andrea Reynolds assumed my value and competence. Then, so did I. Others followed suit. Today, I choose no longer to allow myself to be excluded from humanity by such perceptions I do not share.

(Note to teachers – and we are all teachers: It just takes one. Be that one for someone.)

These days, as awareness of my story grows, folks share their perspectives of me, and my work, daily. Some are hard to hear, while others are beyond gratifying. Which perspectives are real? I learn from them all, so they all are of matter.

Who do you think you are? (Please comment by replying to info@muleandmuseproductions.com)

Really wanting to know,
B

Practical Implications (many of the tips below are revised from my last book, as some teachings are most effective when reviewed):

1. **Be you**. Oscar Wilde wrote, "Be yourself; everyone else is already taken." Humanity needs exactly you. We are just a shade of _____ (readers' choice: "autism," "your name here," "being"… etc… what?) away from unobstructed knowing.
2. **Give us the benefit of the doubt**. Don't assume mental retardation based on behavior and poor communication. One has nothing to lose by assuming competence and treating the different person with non-patronizing respect. Give us the freedom to rise to expectations – surpassing them may come next.
3. **Get to know us.** That should be the first order of business – not trying to fix or change us. Let the autistic person know that

you are there for them and want to get to know who they are and what they do. Everybody has this knowledge about self, although most have it hidden under a bushel. Autistics traditionally have huge bushels weighing down their heads. It is challenging, but all are capable of discovering who they are and what they do. Let it shine.

4. **Listen.** With nonverbal or echolalic autistics, this seems daunting, but break it down. To listen means to make an effort to hear, take notice of, or heed. So, if folks are not talking or typing – observe. Study their past, their proclivities, and how they spend their time. Find out what gives them joy. Once at least one interest is pinpointed, go from there and make learning opportunities and socialization related to that interest. For me, I was interested in history, science, and philosophy. I actually typed that fact many years ago, but that information was enough to get the ball rolling. Through books on tape (yeah, I am that old) and people reading aloud, my curiosity came alive. Next, we slowly incorporated my discussing the readings with Lois or a tutor. To discuss, I had to type, so that increased my mental "on-task time," communication skills, and reason to roll out of bed.

This year, I added podcasts to my learning. Hardcore history (long, scholarly discussions on history) and Professor Buzzkill (brief historical myths explored in humorous ways) are two of my favorites. There is nothing to lose here and much to gain. Podcasts are free, and everyone appreciates being asked what interests them.

5. **Motivate.** Motivation is often tricky for autistics. Curiosity, rather than a burning desire to accomplish, jump-started my internal motivation. As Dorothy Parker wrote, "The cure for boredom is curiosity. There is no cure for curiosity." Make participating in things outside of the autistic mind interesting, safe, and low-stress. Once you entice us out of the autistic mental house, we may find something worth visiting regularly.

6. **Smile.** Smiling is not wasted on autistics. We sense and often take on the affect of those around us. People who are happy,

confident, honest, energetic, and don't take themselves too seriously help make mentally external tasks appealing to us. SS insisted that my team members work with me in only short blocks of time, like two or three hours, to ensure "freshness." Burned-out, tired, listless, disingenuous, or pessimistic workers were not hired.

7. **Be patient.** What normals perceive as "waiting" and "wasting time," we may view as stasis. Like well-seasoned Tibetan monks, we are in no rush. We understand the reality of impermanence. We understand the reality that nothing is as it appears to be. Please, consider here my hypothesis that there are more autistics now because of human evolution. Autism may serve to provide the individual time and space to contemplate and meditate more than any convent or monastery might. Non-verbals "waste no time" on vows of silence. We simply live it.

8. **Persevere**. Set specific goals, both long- and short-term ones. Each day, do at least one thing designed to make progress towards one short-term and one long-term goal. Keep a detailed account of precisely what was accomplished each day. Review this log at the end of each month.

Big Footnote:

Below is a pristine example of the beyond-gratifying kind of comments I get to learn from. (I changed the name for privacy as I did for Dick, but nothing else was altered.)

Dear Barb and Lois –

(I should probably address this to Ms. Rentenbach and Dr. Prislovsky, as I do not know you and deeply respect you. And yet, after reading your wonderfully intimate book, it feels much more appropriate to address you as friends I haven't yet had the pleasure of meeting. So I hope I don't offend you with my greeting.)

I don't know where to start. "Thank you" is probably best, but it seems so woefully inadequate for the emotional roller coaster ride you just took me on as I devoured "I Might Be You" over the past week. I laughed, I cried, I dog-eared pages to come back to, I read whole passages out loud to friends, family and total strangers because I just had to pass these marvelous insights on. I just bought twenty copies to *share with friends, family and the wonderful team of professionals who support our lovely Sonny. I *may* also give one to the a**hole school psychologist who looked at me with condescending pity when I challenged his assessment of my son as mentally retarded. I think IQ tests largely measure our ability to take IQ tests. He thinks I'm in denial. Anyway, I'm not sure he deserves to be let in on the "secret," but I think I'll try anyway for the sake of future children he's asked to "evaluate."*

I am in awe of the mental and physical effort it must have taken to craft this book. I am blown away by the level of raw emotional honesty it required. It is transformative, and even people of your prodigious imaginative powers probably can't imagine the profound impact it is having on all who read it. Thank you. Thank you. A thousand times thank you.

I think one of the most challenging things for a parent is to simultaneously communicate "I love you unconditionally exactly the way you are," AND "I'm going to do all that I can to help you unlock your full potential and help you lead your best life." Your book confirmed for me that it is imperative to keep broadcasting these messages on all channels, and to keep listening ON ALL CHANNELS to what's getting relayed back.

Though I am not nearly as eloquent as either of you, I feel compelled to share something of my own life back with you. This is a poem I wrote a few years ago.

Three Stops on a Long Journey with You
A triptych for Sonny

*"To sing love,
love must first shatter us."
– Angel –*

A trip to my hometown

*I was punch drunk
by the time I went to bed.
You had rained
blows on me
all day.
Fistfuls of hair
lay scattered in the house.
You screamed
for me
to help you.
And I could not.
More than four years
in the trenches
with you.*

Battling.
Inches then yards
of hard-won progress
taken from us
again.
As the loss
of a key weapon
allowed the storm
to surge
in your brain
again.
You kicked
the car so hard
you sprained your ankle.
I watched your little body
limp around the block
as your grandfather
limped behind you.

That night I feared
I would not
sleep.
But I let go
easily
and in my dream
I was swimming
in an ocean lagoon
fins approach
my blood turns icy
I cannot reach the shore
the warm salt water roils
inches from me
a dolphin breaks the surface.
A dolphin,
I marvel.
I touch,
the smooth skin
is soothing.
It clicks at me
and stays by my side.

In the morning when I wake
I remember

with the sharpness of memory
rather than haziness of sleep.
I turn it over
in my mind
not sure
if I am convincing myself
that it is
or is not
a sign
a message from the universe
or god
or my own reeling subconscious
something that loves me
whispering a message
"Don't be afraid"
or
"Remember
some profoundly intelligent
life forms communicate
without words"
or
"Something will come
and help you
swim to shore".
I know that it's just
a random synapse
firing in my brain
but just for today
I want to believe
it is a sign.
I want to believe
something.

A trip to the park

Crunching our way through the tidy
piles of brilliantly hued leaves
you are shouting
"Shaw wa wee!"
at max volume
in the otherwise quiet neighborhood.
I follow you
like an uncertain echo

and am rewarded
with a smile
and then a bubbling laugh.
We wind our way
through the streets
in a slow crescendo,
happy.
A couple approaches
from the opposite direction
puzzled, then dazzled
by the fierce joy
you are flinging
at the piercing blue October sky.
The man catches your
fleeting eye – no small feat –
and shouts
"Sha wa wee!"
right back at you.
Startled still for a moment
a smile explodes across your face
transfiguring you
with a violent beauty.
We stare at you, stunned,
as if witnessing
the apparition of an angel
from the age of miracles.
I want to weep my thanks
to these strangers
for their casual kindness.
Instead I smile
and we continue to the park
where we fight about your shoes.
Later at home
you tell me "Sit"
and push me
onto the orange couch.
Though only a head
shorter than me
you climb onto my lap
and bury your face
in my neck
then raise your head
and say "Hug."

A trip to the zoo

Sunday at the zoo
I try vainly
to get you to stop
for a moment
and look at the lions
or giraffes
or playful otters.
But we just race
around the crowded paths
hardly glancing
at the exotic inhabitants
and then finish our circuit
with the usual beeline
to the primate house
where you will spend
more than half an hour,
longer than you do
just about anything else,
in front of the gorillas.
You'll push your way
just in front of the biggest one
as I whisper hurried apologies
behind you.
Though he seemed impassive
as we approached
I swear he stares
back at you.
Something about the quiet symmetry
unnerves me still,
the way you seem to share
an intelligence so orthogonal
to the one that prevails
in the surrounding world.
As I think about the thousands
of hours of therapy
and the halting words –
a couple hundred?
at your command.
I wonder
if we have made
nearly as much progress

on our own road
to meet you.
I try to keep my face impassive
but I can tell
by the pained looks
of passers by
that I have not succeeded.
I hate the zoo.

I'll stop there, know that you, of all people, know the inadequacy of words to express what I am trying to say. Thanks again.

Very truly yours,

Angel
P.S. If you are still in touch with Jess Wilson of A Diary of a Mom, please thank her for me for introducing me to your book via her blog!
Angel

And that, my friends, is the circular joy of giving.
Enjoy the beautiful poetry above and all around.
B

EF happily connecting and communicating through objects.

Chapter 12

Using Objects as Communication Bridges
for ASD and ADHD
by Lois Prislovsky

"Too often we forget that discipline really means to teach, not to punish. A disciple is a student, not a recipient of behavioral consequences." Daniel Siegel

{NOTE TO READER = I shared with Barb my concerns that this chapter is long and tedious. Barb typed, "True, you are no Dr. Andrew Solomon, but I guess the fashion police already ticketed you for that. Folks will benefit from these simple truths. I'll insert random fun, like an interrupting turtle, to help the medicine go down. You present the ideas, leave the sidekicks to me." Helpful B}

Part One: Autism Spectrum Disorder (ASD)

I have been doing a post-doc at Barb Rentenbach University for over ten years. As a generous thinker and non-verbal woman with autism **(Helpful B: "You should also mention my thick, silky hair."),** Barb has taught me a great deal – perhaps most importantly that there is no gold-standard brain. Just as (despite the Standard Poodle lobbyists' claims) there is no standard dog, no standard flower, no standard culture or race. Diversity of brains, like biodiversity, is by design.

Let's examine what Barb typed as a comment on Ariane Zurcher's outstanding blog (Emma's Hope) about how many individuals with autism communicate better through typing.

Barb: Speaking vs. typing
"Emma typed, "language is an awkward way to communicate" – and I argue that this is true for everyone, but highly challenging for

those of us who are autistically wired. It took me years to think in language. But prior to that, my thinking was not faulty; it was just not language based. Thinking in language is not efficient for me. I wish I could give you a pretty little fact package about what works, so that folks like me could get such treatment and soar socially and academically. Of course, the problem is... it is hard to say in language. Typing makes it way easier, because I can control the speed of each thought and break it down into smaller parts, to be better described by letters one peck at a time. Speaking requires a rather unnatural process for me – perhaps like you singing a song you heard in another language. You may be able to imitate the sounds, but the meaning in each mimic is not precise. The best way for me now is to communicate through typing. But still my thinking is not easily translated into words. Feelings, sensations, visions and knowings that are cleanly processed in my mind don't fit well into letter symbols. There, I said it – or something close. Thanks for caring. Trying B"

We know that many with ASD often relate better to objects than people. One of the first books I read on the subject was Donna Williams's (1992) *Nobody Nowhere: The Extraordinary Autobiography of an Autistic.* Williams explains that, "Communication via objects was safe."

The computer is an object that may be a bridge to interpersonal connection and growth. So the very day that Barb typed the above comment, I read it aloud (with Barb's permission) to two adult, non-verbal clients who struggle with "severe autism." In their separate sessions, they smiled and understood immediately.

Both men started typing that day.

These gentlemen (one in his early thirties and the other recently turned sixty) were mostly non-verbal, but could say "yes" and "no." They appeared to have well-developed receptive language, but barely any expressive language save a few random phrases. The men were from different families and backgrounds. But both were institutionalized and were brought to see me for weekly sessions, because someone in their family read Barb's book and had hope. Each of these clients also listened to her book, either via audiobook or by having someone read it aloud to them.

Barb is good for business – very good.

(Helpful B: "True, sex sells")

That day these gentlemen began to type and say their "yes" and "no" answers as they typed the words – on their own. A few minutes later, each man moved on to typing letter answers to multiple-choice questions, which really opened up learning, connections, and taking initiatives to communicate preferences and opinions.

We are seeing clients like these make gains years faster than Barb did and with significantly less one-on-one session time, because she gives such precise accounts of what worked for her and WHY. Her recipes are not hard to follow.

(Helpful B: "Plus I'm less fattening and more diversity friendly than Paula Deen.")

Presumed competence is always the foundation. Barb emphasizes talking as little as possible when establishing connection with people who struggle with language. **(Helpful B: "I actually said who struggle with LUGGAGE, but either way – we are smart. Please shut up and help.")** Also, respectfully observing how much physical space from others they prefer, and mirroring some movement, is usually appreciated. For example, the sixty year old, whom I will call E.F., has many harmless, obsessive-compulsive rituals that ease his anxiety. He always spins three times when exiting my office. I wordlessly spin with him. That always makes E.F. smile. Me too.

In our practice, every practitioner emails detailed daily session notes so that the specifics of care will be replicable. Below is an actual session note from E.F.'s work, two months after the aforementioned typing breakthrough. E.F. gave his permission, as did his sister who was his conservator at the time of this writing. You will note that the font we use in working with E.F. is size eighteen – Barb taught us that, too, plus the man is sixty. We keep it all capitals to match the letters on the keyboard, to help E.F. make fewer translation steps.

What a wonderful session. E.F. was all smiles, and cooperative for the duration. His typing and self-generated speech have improved significantly. Please see below for details. = 1 session

LP = WOULD YOU LIKE TO START PRACTICING SPEECH WITH PICTURES, STORY CUBES, OR OBJECTS THAT YOU DON'T SEE?

EF = SAID "PICTURES"

LP = I BROUGHT A "BEST OF LIFE MAGAZINE" COFFEE TABLE BOOK – SOME OF THE IMAGES ARE WAR TORN AND EMOTIONAL. IS THAT OKAY?

EF = (SAID "OKAY," CLEARLY)

(E.F. spoke what he saw in the picture. He sometimes needed a prompt, like, "Wilt the ____". After he spoke each word, I typed it on the screen. Then E.F. typed it and repeated it aloud again. He typed this on his own. I was not touching him. I simply typed this on my laptop and then handed the computer to him, he then typed his phrase after seeing what I had typed. This was how he put it all together; letter by letter – sound by sound in a multimodal approach. He appeared to be making these learning connections at that very moment. For example, when he saw Muhammad Ali on the screen he said, "Ali" and then I typed "Muhammad Ali". He then typed "Muhammad Ali", saying each letter aloud as he typed it while I said each letter after him- followed by how it sounded. He then repeated the entire word or phrase. E.F. also put each sound and letter together as I tapped out the syllables on his arm to help E.F. get a cadence for more "natural speech." He was open to it and began speaking those connections.)

FIRE
FIRE
GRAVE
GRAVE
SAILOR KISSING
SAILOR KISSING
GUARD DOGS
GUARD DOGS

JACK RUBY KILLS
JACK RUBY KILLS (HE READ AND SAID THE FULL
SENTENCE!!! MR. EF, YOU ARE SPEAKING!)

WILT THE STILT
WILT THE STILT
MUHAMMAD ALI
MUHAMMAD ALI
(WHEN WE TAP OUT SYLLABLES, EF's SPEAKING IS SO
VERY CLEAR. GREAT WORK LOTS OF SMILES!)
CHURCHILL ROOSEVELT STALIN
CHURCHILL ROOSEVELT STALIN

LP = DO YOU WANT TO DO SOUND CLIPS OR OBJECTS
NEXT? (Objects are a variety bag of items I keep in my office for the
client to hold under the table and take out one thing at a time without
looking at it so they may verbalize what they feel. This technique also
helps my clients with sensory integration issues.)

EF = (SAID "OBJECTS" LOUD AND CLEAR)

LP = REMEMBER PLEASE JUST HOLD THEM UNDER THE
TABLE AND SAY WHAT YOU THINK IT IS BEFORE YOU
LOOK AT IT. OK?

EF = (SAID "YES")

"WATCH" = (HE SAID IT WITHOUT LOOKING AT IT!)

"PAINT BRUSH" = (AGAIN – EF NAMED THE ITEM JUST BY
FEELING IT UNDER THE TABLE!)

"SPOON" = (HE IS 3 FOR 3 SAYING IT BY JUST FEELING THE
OBJECT.)

"NECKLACE" = (EF NEEDED TO BRING THIS ONE UP TO SEE – BUT STILL SAID ON HIS OWN.)

"MATCHES" = (DID NOT NAME THIS ONE CORRECTLY – PERHAPS DUE TO LACK OF EXPOSURE.)

"IT'S A SCREW" = (WOW, FULL SENTENCE CORRECT!)

"KEY" = (CORRECT AGAIN WITH JUST TOUCH.)

"CARD" = (CORRECT!)

LP = WOULD YOU LIKE TO DO SOUND CLIPS OR PICTURE CUBES NOW?

EF = SAID "SOUND CLIPS"

(I played these sounds from a free app called iButton. He spoke it. I typed it. And then E.F. typed it again saying every letter and space as he typed. Then E.F. said it a few more times for practice. This connection had him use all his senses in a multimodal approach to learning how to speak and type simultaneously.)
ROCKY
ROCKY
SEXY AND I KNOW IT
SEXY AND I KNOW IT
SHOTGUN
SHOTGUN
THAT WAS EASY
THAT WAS EASY
TWILIGHT ZONE
TWILIGHT ZONE
WOODY WOODPECKER LAUGH
WOODY WOODPECKER LAUGH
(I TYPED IT OUT AFTER HE SAID IT INITIALLY AFTER HEARING THE SOUND AND THEN HE RETYPED IT ON HIS

OWN SAYING EVERY LETTER AND THEN READING THE WHOLE PHRASE)

EF = "CAN WE GO?"

LP = YES. I DO WANT TO KNOW IF YOU WANT TO LISTEN TO BARB'S RADIO SHOW ON YOUR IPAD AT YOUR HOUSE?

EF = SAID "NO. CAN WE GO? CAN WE GO?"

LP = BEFORE YOU GO PLEASE TELL ME WHAT YOU ENJOYED THE MOST.
PICTURES, OBJECTS, OR SOUNDS

EF = "SOUNDS YES" "CAN WE GO? CAN WE GO?"

With his permission, we frequently took pictures and videos of E.F.'s progress to send along with his session notes. His very impressed sisters also came in to observe him working. E.F. now reads hundreds of sight words and has a vocabulary in the thousands. Barb was right. **(Helpful B: You're right too – this is long and tedious."**)

I should also note that these are not fancy techniques that must be administered by a high-dollar expert. **(Helpful B: "Whom do I talk to about a refund?")** In fact, since E.F. was on a limited budget, we let CJ, one of our college-aged ASD aides, sit in on a few sessions and then do the same kind of practice with E.F. at his residential facility on Saturdays at a fraction of the cost.

In *The Power of Habit: Why We Do What We Do In Life and Business*, Charles Duhigg deciphers what these dear clients were able to do: "Habits can be changed if we understand how they work... you must keep the old cue, and deliver the old reward, but insert a new routine." E.F. had had years of speech therapy to no real gain. We inserted a new multimodal routine. When he shifted his routine, he was able to build on that. E.F. shifted his learning routine by adding objects that he himself chose for his communication practice.

Here is a list of objects E.F. enjoyed using to practice spontaneous speech and independent typing.

1. iPad = He came to us well known for his love of drawing pictures on his iPad drawing application. We built on this affinity, starting with letters. I would type a letter on my laptop keyboard, then E.F. would draw that letter on his iPad. We did this non-verbally. Soon, E.F. trusted me enough to allow me to draw a few letters on his iPad, then he would erase it and draw the same letters himself. Next, we played the same wordless drawing game with a "wingding" font (non-alphabet symbols) that I enlarged and displayed on my computer. We took turns selecting a wingding symbol from the laptop screen and drawing it on his iPad. Each person took turns copying the other's drawing. This simple give-and-take game – where our skills were comparable – opened the door for E.F. to try new things at every visit.
2. Scrabble tiles – all capital letters. We often used these as an alternative to typing or drawing letters.
3. Dice – another, more active way to practice saying numbers with no verbal or boring two-dimensional prompts. (My son Eli would like you to know that pixels have depth, but you get my point.) We soon moved on to the game Yahtzee, which can be played perfectly without speaking… save for the "Yahtzee!" scream.
4. TV clips from '70s sitcoms – found easily on YouTube. E.F. now types into the search bar the name of the show clip he wishes to view, and then talks briefly about it.
5. Story cubes – a small box of twenty-one dice-like cubes with a different picture on each of the six sides (126 images for practicing quick, spontaneous speech).
6. Large-print encyclopedias with color pictures (this same content can be found online by simply zooming in and enlarging the font accompanying each picture.)
7. ACT and SAT vocabulary cards with picture cues.

8. Random objects I keep in a bag to help clients with sensory-integration issues. I place the object under the table and hand it to the client, who then names the object without looking.
9. Brief (two- to three-minute) videos of topics of interest to E.F. – such as CNN, science, or MUSIC! E.F. often chooses rap music, classics from the '70s and '80s, and anything upbeat from Elvis.
10. Audiobooks – played in five- to ten-minute chunks, then "discussed."
11. Sound clips from iButton (free app)

Part Two: Attention Deficit Hyperactivity Disorder (ADHD)

That idea about using objects as communication bridges worked so well, I decided to try it with a very impulsive ADHD client who is intellectually gifted but struggles mightily with anxiety and anger. The plan was to use typing to require him to use more areas of his brain before he communicates impulsively.

G.H. is a slight twelve-year-old who got expelled from school two days before this session with me for refusing to do the work and distracting others. Now, getting expelled from public middle school usually involves more – Lindsay Lohan or Mike Tyson kind of more. But my guy was motivated. G.H. wanted to be home-schooled for a variety of tween reasons, so he calculated that his crimes could not be of the level to get him sent away, but must be significant enough for a decisive and early departure. With Special Forces-like precision to avoid collateral damage (G.H. likes his peers and wants them to like him), he targeted a teacher who he calculated would quickly take him to their leader. Then, using only clean SAT word weapons, he was extracted before lunch. Told you he was smart.

My plan was much simpler: Have G.H. type to be more mindful of what he communicates.

I wordlessly greeted the family in the lobby and led them back to my office, then started typing. (**Helpful B: "Wordless greetings are my favorite, especially when accompanied by bread baskets."**) We passed the laptop back and forth to communicate. I enlarged the font so his parents could read our conversation from the couch where they were sitting, as G.H. and I worked at a nearby table. Periodically the parents and I would speak, as we can be trusted to be measured and honest with our speech, but G.H. was only to communicate through typing that day as his impulsive and angry words had been causing too much hurt of late. He was empowered with a voice and could even interrupt if he chose, but his input would only be acknowledged through structured typing.

(Helpful B: "If I find out this is some experiment on me, somebody's gonna get bitten.")

Here are a few excerpts from the session transcript:

LP = we are going to communicate today a little differently. we are going to slow down our communications by typing. your words have been hurting you and others, so we are going to talk today by typing.

GH = okay

LP = good. let's start by you imagining the man you want to be for ten seconds. okay?

GH = Fine you seem mad r u mad ?

LP = no I am not angry or mad. I am not impressed with your choices of late. how do you feel?

(Out of respect, we redacted GH's very angry response. It is not his baseline.)

LP = OKAY! VERY clear! Excellent mature and honest communication and control. we are hearing you loud and clear. now, to find out what is wrong. when one hurts, it's usually because something in you is not as it should be. you have a thought?

(Btw thank you very much for being so calm, and not interrupting)
(Helpful B: "Is she talking to me? Now I am confused. Is ADHD contagious?")

(G.H.'s private response again redacted as not relevant to this example.)

LP = oh, actually my point in communicating like this today was not to punish. **I learned that typing helps people be less impulsive, and more mindful of each statement, because it forces one to slow down and really think through something.** *you have just demonstrated patience, maturity, and lots of non-silly, truthful answers. This is the way I would like to hear from you today. So if you need a break, please rest while I speak with your parents. If you want to say something, please type it. We will listen. My rules. My office. Understood?*

GH = yes
IM SORRY. I DID WHAT I DID. CAN YOU focus on helping me fix this!!!!!!!!!!!!!

[END of session excerpt]

It worked!

G.H.'s impulsiveness and non-truthful responses dropped dramatically. This precious young man responded beautifully to this novel structure. For the first time in our many sessions together, G.H. was fully present, attentive, honest, and respectful for the full hour.

G.H. was able to slow down and process from another perspective and area of his brain. Then he was able to reflect in this mirror that typing revealed. G.H. began to see how he was perceived, and it was not in line with his true self, which caused distress. His anger dissipated and he became more mindful about being the good apple that he is.

I used this same technique with another hyperverbal ADHD client, who also suffered from social anxiety and poor peer relationships. Fourteen-year-old I.J. spoke in extended, rushed prose that often got so tangential it was difficult to discern his true thoughts and feelings. Typing also slowed this teenager down enough to become more selective and authentic about what he chose to communicate. Individuals with ADHD often think best when moving – and motion, coupled with less word diarrhea, cleared I.J.'s focus to produce refreshing introspection and honesty. Another benefit was that before I.J. practiced give-and-take typing conversations with me, he was perceived as arrogant and off-putting with his monopolizing style of primarily self-centered talking. Typing conversations quickly taught I.J. natural breaks, and he was forced to be quiet while the other person typed. I.J. was soon able to translate this format to verbal communications. I.J.'s conversational social skills improved dramatically, because he was now able to break down how to cooperate with another person.

Multimodal communication requires more diverse brain real-estate and thus makes strong, novel connections for fresh learning.

"If you have an apple and I have an apple and we exchange these apples, then you and I will still each have one apple. But if you have an idea and I have an idea and we exchange these ideas, then each of us will have two ideas." George Bernard Shaw

SS and me laughing on air with LOUD MUTE RADIO. Considered loud mute worker B

Chapter 13
One Loud, Proud Mute
by Barb Rentenbach

"Synergy is better than **my way** or **your way**. It's **our way**." – Stephen R. Covey

I am so proud of myself these days. I know that sounds arrogant, even coming from a person who does not make reliable sounds. But, my emotion is clear and I think sharing it may inspire others to persevere with being themselves. So I will risk being considered egotistical, as it sure beats not being considered.

Below is an excerpt of what I typed as my goals in 2012. (Our beloved marketing strategist, Jennifer Ho-Dougatz, requires this before she agrees to take on a new client.)

My Ultimate Vision:
"Be a writer and producer. Known for wit, wisdom, and generosity. Be married. Travel extensively with my loving husband... and personal attendant (for all my untidy needs) so Mr. Right and I can keep the positive energy and mutual respect. Support myself and staff financially for as long as we all shall live. **_Legacy_** _= Helen Keller-like inspiration, but with Mark Twain humor and publications that last. I plan on writing many books in myriad genres, each creatively unique in process and form. SS and I will do all projects together, feeding off each other's strengths and enjoying ourselves immensely. "Autism Advocate" will not be my only title; eventually, my musings will inspire mainstreamers – and that will serve my ASD clan best. My work and person will change ASD inside and outside."_

– I am a writer. (Tah Dah! Please read on.)
– I am a producer. (Ever heard of LOUD MUTE RADIO? It is a Mule and **MUSE production**.)

– I am in a long-term relationship. Please see the picture of my tall, handsome, engineer boyfriend, Jerry, in this thirteen-page cover-story spread about "my success" in Zoom Autism Magazine at www.zoomautism.org.
– My writing was just used in a beautiful eulogy, for Noelle, written by Jess Wilson and shared with hundreds of thousands in her wildly popular "Diary of a Mom" blog. Folks keep eulogies… so that counts as lasting.

I was also featured on a *Big Girl Panties* podcast episode about humor, wisdom, and generosity, which checks off several of my goals and was more fun than one is supposed to have at work.

It is nice to show growth that does not involve buying larger clothes – only a little bigger hat.

But success does not happen overnight, or without daily fight.

The hardest thing I ever had to do was learn to type independently. I fought doing it for years. I still struggle with the infuriating level of difficulty and slowness. But I know it must be accomplished to do my part to help make neurodiversity workers be as common as juice stains in minivans.

In these blog highlights below that I wrote on August 6th, 2014, I chronicle some of my starter steps:

October is National Disability Employment Awareness Month. For once, I am performing ahead of schedule.

Mule and Muse Productions (a fancy name for Lois and me, respectively) just signed a contract with Hangar Studios, NYC, to produce podcasts.

I am officially a working stiff – albeit a rather doughy one.

The "Ask Barb" part of the show needs your help. (How did you think having a mute on the air would work? Radio silence disappeared with the Cold War.)

Please submit any question you like – preferably ones you are too afraid or polite to ask someone with autism. Ratings, people! You know I will pick the titillating stuff for the show. I do not know everything about autism, but I promise to be an open book – and believe me I will have an opinion, no matter the topic.

Healing is the process of making sound again – and the reason this mute is in radio.

I imagine being heard. I imagine you being heard.

The beauty of this mission is that we must work together. True muse style.

In order to share light, others must be inspired to illuminate their aptitudes and passions.

Over the next months, I will recruit talent to feature and fill all supporting roles.

The surface rarely reveals the richest Human Resources. Screw the status quo environment – I plan to drill, baby, drill.

The US Department of Labor cites that only 17.6 % of persons with a disability are employed. It's time to do the Civil Rights swing. I plan to discriminate. Individuals with disabilities will be given preference, and probably complimentary drinks and other cool swag. Bye bye, ableism – see ya, wouldn't want to be ya.

Projects thrive with neurodiversity, and I am not afraid to type it.

Not fair? Really? Please get in line. Did you know there is a loophole in our nation's head, making it legal to pay people with disabilities less than the minimum wage? Jess Wilson's brilliant article on her blog, entitled "Good Will," highlights this wrong truth.

Thank you for being open to changing your mind and the world through equality and listening up.

Not sub-human or sub-minimum-wage, B

Practical Implications:

1. Healing is the process of making sound again, and again and again. My first Loud Mute Radio show was a peak experience for me. My learning and connecting grows with each podcast. My favorite ninja guest, Sensei Nadine Champion, taught me about courage and shared the writings of Mark Nepo, the author of *The Book of The Awakening* and *Seven Thousand Ways to Listen: Staying Close to What is Sacred*. Nepo reminds us that if there are 7,000 languages and ways to speak, there must be that many ways to listen. I plan to learn from them all.

"If I dare hear you, I will feel like the sun and grow in your direction." Mark Nepo

2. Courage and connection are needed to give all gifts, and this is our collective purpose.
3. I share the healing power of being heard. We are all each other's cure. God cares about us all through us all.

While researching synthetic biology for the show, I learned that a "muton" is the smallest unit of DNA at which a change can occur. Thanks for turning this mute on.

Ty and me out on the town on our wedding day. The black and white photo helps conceal how much better young Marylin looked on a similar air vent. By the time we were allowed to marry, I did not look like a blushing bride much less Marylin Monroe but it is hard to blame the latter that on the slow wheels of justice. (The Supreme Court takes even longer than the DMV.) True story: Fashionable friends took me dress shopping for the big event and as I entered the first store and was asked if I needed help I said, "Yes please, I need a wedding dress." The fancy shop lady immediately gushed, "Oh, yes! Mother of the Bride – Right this way!" Oh well, I am just happy to taste the rainbow without getting shot.

Chapter 14

DMV – That's so Gay

by Lois Prislovsky

"Harold knew that the higher up he went, the farther he could see. So he decided to make the hill into a mountain."

That quotation is from Crockett Johnson's *Harold and the Purple Crayon*. It is my wife Ty's favorite children's book. (Okay. That is not exactly true. Her favorite children's book is Jack Kent's *Socks for Supper*. *Harold and the Purple Crayon* is the children's book that most reminds Ty of me... so it is very high on her list.) All the things Harold draws come true.

This morning that book was on my nightstand. I don't know why. This morning is Sunday. Ty works on the weekends, so we awoke early for me to make her favorite food in the world – French-press coffee. I make it impressively strong, like Ty.

Last night, Ty could tell that something was weighing on my mind. This morning I was ready to tell someone. Lucky Ty. Lucky you.

Eli turned fifteen last month. Every Saturday of that month, I woke him early and got him to and from a "Drive for Life" class, from 8:30 am to 5 pm. For his short lunch break, I brought Eli his favorite foot-long sandwich from Subway (Philly cheese steak with mozzarella, jalapenos, oil and vinegar, and a smattering of lettuce to remind him that he is still mortal and colon cancer is real and so is his Mom). He had everything he needed. I have seen to that every day since before he was born. (My dissertation was titled "The Effects of Prenatal Stimulation on Human Cognitive Development," so Eli got an extra-early start.)

This Friday was the big day – Eli was getting his driver's permit. DMV hours are basically school hours, with about thirty more enigmatic holiday closures thrown in just to keep citizens knowing who is boss. Timing was critical. He was out of school for parent-teacher conferences, so I took the day off. After the conference, I got his sleeping-in self out of bed and happily off to the DMV.

Weeks prior, I had gathered the considerable documents needed: Birth Certificate, SS #, Proof of Tennessee residency (mail with his name on it), Form SF1010 from school stating that he is attending and I am his parent (must be thirty days current… we were on day twenty-one), Certification from Drive for Life stating that Eli passed the written test, and here is the biggie for this discussion – TEENAGE AFFIDAVIT/FINANCIAL RESPONSIBILITY – "If guardian or step-parent is not named on school attendance (**I am**): proof of relationship will be required such as custody or adoption papers or marriage certificate if step-parent is signing."

The DMV line was not that bad. Eli's cousin was just ahead of us, and we had a friendly chat on this exciting day. His cousin, who did not take a Drive for Life class so he still had to take a DMV written test, got his permit in about thirty-five minutes. It took us over four hours. Here is why:

Bureaucrat #1: "This won't work. You are not listed as the mother on the birth certificate."

Me: "Right. We asked the nurse, but she refused to list me as the other parent on the birth certificate. She said, 'You are not the father, and in Tennessee we only list the mother and father – if known.' Our dear donor is known, but chooses to be anonymous."

Bureaucrat #1: "Then your name needs to be a hyphenated last name."

Me = "That was our plan, and we asked that too. Again the nurse refused, saying, 'No. You two are not married.' Which of course was not allowed either. So the best we could do was put my last name as his middle name. As you see, that was done."

Bureaucrat #1: "Then you need to show me adoption papers."

Me: "We tried that too, but adoption in Tennessee was not possible without stripping the other parent of her rights."

Bureaucrat #1: "Okay, just show me proof of guardianship."

Me: "Here are the school records, which identify me as one of Eli's Parent/Guardians."

Bureaucrat #1: "That does not count."

Me: "We also had this Co-parenting legal agreement drawn up and notarized before he was born." (I hand it to her, still managing a patient smile.)

Bureaucrat #1: "We need the original. This copy has the father's name redacted. I need to make copies of the original."

Me: "Correct. The donor chooses to be anonymous, and we respect that and are forever grateful for his gift. But he signed all legal rights to this child over to me and Eli's other Mom. All that is clearly stated in this notarized co-parenting agreement, signed by all three of us."

Bureaucrat #2 joins in the fun and studies the co-parenting agreement: "A judge did not even sign this."

Me: "True. We paid the counsel of two top civil-rights attorneys – one in Knoxville and one in Nashville. Both advised us to do the co-parenting agreement and wait till the law catches up. Both said that no sitting judge at the time would sign it. I paid to check again a few years ago and that is still the case."

Bureaucrat #2: "Right. So it is not legal. You are not his legal parent."

Me: (Okay, this is starting to REALLY hurt. But, my boy is here and this is about what he needs, not me. I mentally forgive her immediately, and choose persistence over victimhood... imploring the hot water swelling behind my stinging eyes to get with my program.) "It was the best we could do. I appreciate you both listening to this and trying to help. You see we are trying to go by the rules every step. May I please speak to your supervisor?"

Bureaucrat #1: "Wait over there."

Time passes. I feel the eyes and ears of many curious Tennesseans. I mentally bless them all. Patient but hungry Eli somehow grows taller. If embarrassed or put out by my mini-Rosa Parks slow ride, he did not show it. I love him even more. I try to be gracious but steadfast, knowing we are being overheard and considered by many who may have never considered this before. They are putting a face to the issue. I do my best to be a good face, but I am getting so tired of the same fight, arena after arena.

Manager, Bureaucrat #3 arrives. His shirt is on but he looks and sounds like Vladimir Putin, and he has an alphabet soup name like mine. We learn later that his name is Marc and he is Czech. We like him. I can tell he likes us too. Eli, blond, blue-eyed, six foot three, looks like a prized countryman. And Marc is respectful to me.

Marc and I repeat the conversation above. (Incidentally, I had an almost identical conversation earlier this week with two phone bureaucrats when we misplaced Eli's birth certificate and I tried to order a new copy. After two and a half hours of being my best phone face, I was also denied. But they did hear me out. Fortunately, we found the birth certificate. Not having access to your government, which you fund, is humiliating. We keep going because there is no alternative and it will be easier for the next family.)

Me: "What would you have me do differently?"

Manager Bureaucrat #3 "Have the other parent sign this form and have it notarized, and bring it back." (Marc is now using the words "other parent," and even says to Eli, "I want you to be able to drive your Mom home." His compassion is pure love.)

Me: "Okay, I can leave and come back with that. (It is now almost 2 pm and they close at 5 pm The line is now literally out the door.) What does that document say?"

Manager Bureaucrat #3: "It says she assumes all financial responsibility and gives permission for Eli to get his drivers permit."

Me: "That is a problem, because we split up when Eli was four. So, Eli divides his time between our two homes. I am the primary breadwinner, and thus I assume Eli's car, insurance, and all financial responsibilities."

Manager Bureaucrat #3: "Let me get my supervisor. Please wait here."

(Time passes. It is embarrassingly insulting to be told, "You are not his real parent" – when you know you are. Eli is hanging in there. Now, I am beginning to double-check my motives. Am I being selfish? Pushy? Dramatic? Our boy just wants his permit. Why don't I just let his birthmother take him on another day? Wait, here comes the BIG Supervisor...)

Supervising Bureaucrat #4: (We repeat the same conversation. In Bill Murray's movie *Groundhog Day*, Phil, the protagonist, makes minor adjustments to try and change the outcome each time the day is re-played. I refuse to change the script – because my plan is complete honesty. As Barb says, I am "stupidly honest." I am confident that when people know better they do better. The best I can do is to connect with each person who is listening.)

Supervising Bureaucrat #4: (She listened and then repeated the party line.)

Me: "Thank you for your time and for listening. We will go get his Mother." (We agreed on what Eli would call us before he was born. She chose "Mommy" and I chose Mom. I anticipated the limited shelf life on "Mommy"... but his transition to "Mother" was easy enough... although it often makes Eli sound like he is in the theater.)

Manager Bureaucrat #3: "You don't have to stand in line again. Please just come through the side door and ask for Marc." (Another beautiful gift from a kind, blue-eyed, blond man.)

Eli and Me: "Oh, thank you!"

I asked Eli to call Mommy on his phone because I knew she would pick up. She did, and said, "Oh, I have to drive all the way to Strawberry Plains?" We said we would come get her. Eli calls her house Base 1 and our house "The Pink House" – everybody does – it's not a gay slur... or maybe it is, but that works too, as the current and previous owners share DMV issues. And our house is literally painted pink.

Forty minutes later we arrive at Base 1. She was ready, and offered to follow us so I would not have to drive her back. She was very gracious. With Marc's side-door support, Eli was able to get his permit – eleven minutes before closing.

Eli drove me home.

This story does not end there. Later that night, I dropped Eli off at a bowling alley for a double date with his girlfriend and two classmates. I had two hours to kill. I began to analyze the day's events.

On the car ride to Base 1, when Mommy said, "Oh, I have to drive all the way to Strawberry Plains?" that pissed me off. But, I could not decide if I was angry or disappointed. And she was being nothing but helpful – so I was not angry with her. In fact, it was more a revelation. Emotions like anger and disappointment are not intrinsically bad. In fact, they are often pristine indicators that change is needed.

When I got off the phone with her, I told Eli why I think "Habitat for Humanity" is so successful. (He is used to tangentially related conversations with me.) I said, "People who get these homes have to work very hard – a minimum of 500 hours of 'sweat equity' – and pay mortgages too, albeit affordable mortgage payments due to volunteer construction help, along with no-profit sales, and 0% interest loans. So, most Habitat owners take exceptional care of their homes, and do not take them for granted, because they were hard earned."

"Eli, being gay is not a pain in the ass (avoiding a raunchy tired joke) – it is a pain in the heart. Many straight people often take being a parent for granted, and thus complain about some of what is required as a parent. Son, please never take being a parent for granted. Live it as an honor and a privilege, and your children will cherish the value of your relationship."

I see now that thanks to this type of consistent extra effort to be validated as a "real parent," I can honestly say that, with regards to Eli, I have no regrets. I am far from perfect. But every single day, since before he was born, I give Eli my best.

I don't want this chapter to be received as a complaint. When we complain, we choose the role of victim. I wish that role on no one.

It is simply a true story that I hope inspires compassionate use of your purple crayon.

Addendum – four months later:

(I typed it in later, but originally I wrote this addendum by hand – because it felt so firsthandedly personal.)

On this morning's jog, while I listened to a podcast about synesthesia, my audio lesson was interrupted by this text, "HRC ALERT: SCOTUS rules marriage bans unconstitutional, marriage equality for all!"

So never mind... we fixed it.

As Arianna Huffington says, "Life is about how quickly we course-correct." So, I plan to get right to it and find joyous ways to spend that extra $489 a month we currently pay on separate insurance, since my wife's company can no longer refuse to cover our family. I guess I should also let Eli know he is not really a bastard anymore, except when he leaves sticky mint-chocolate ice cream bowls in his room. Whenever I hear the word "bastard," it reminds me of my best friend Gina and our favorite line from Mark Vonnegut's book, *The*

Eden Express, "And the bastard got closer and closer, as bastards always do." Thank God.

And thank those of you who helped draw those equal purple lines.

Flying high with my niece Augusta, nephew John, Smother (Barbara Rentenbach), DD ("Dearest Dad"/Mike Rentenbach), and big brother, Tim Rentenbach. Intentionally happily employed B

Chapter 15

Revolution

by Barb Rentenbach

"All our dreams can come true if we have the courage to pursue." Walt Disney

Much energy has been spent debating what to call folks with neurologies similar to mine. My honorable friend Jess Wilson, of *Diary of a Mom* fame, wrote a politically correct and concise blog about the controversy, and has chosen, "unless and until Brooke directs me otherwise, to follow the Autistic community's lead in using identity-first language (*i.e. to say, 'Brooke is autistic,'* vs. *'Brooke has autism.'*)."

My opinion is this:
"Dear Jess, Our words matter, but our actions may matter more. On Loud Mute Radio, my loyal SS often says "individuals with autism labels" to make it better. But what really makes it better is that she genuinely respects me, and what I offer, so we are in legitimate business together – fifty-fifty partners. Personally (key word: person) not too concerned with labels, B"

Most would think I am unemployable. As more than luck would have it, I found a mule in need of a muse – so I own Mule and Muse Productions, LLC, with SS. Our company produces books, presentations, and podcasts (quite a trick for mutes – so always worth the price of admission.) Like Plato, I know we are born whole but need each other to complete ourselves.

When I discovered that autism is my prism, not my prison, my career path began to reveal itself. Response to *I Might Be You: An Exploration of Autism and Connection* was overwhelmingly positive, and it led many precious readers to ask me questions regarding autism. This was new to me and showed me more of my potential.

You see, being disguised as a poor thinker, people don't don't ask my advice. They never have. Ask one of my bull-dyke lesbian friends about wedding dress fashion and you will get the same surprise. It's simply not expected. No one does it.

But Paula Deens: be on notice. Times have changed.

Like my dear queers who now enjoy marriage equality, this is new to me – and thrilling – so my lifeline finger is working overtime. It is still not enough, so my clever publicist suggested we start an "Ask Barb" column to be more efficient with frequently asked questions. My weary, but proud, finger and I accept her proposal.

The beauty of asking a mute is that the answers will sound familiar, as the voice is yours.

The plan is to help folks sculpt themselves with intention. This is not a one-way street, as learning never is. You see, even on a modest day, I claim to know a ton about my kind of autism. Forty-three years of studying my wacky neuronal firings, and experimenting with navigating my autistic landscape, earned me an honorary Ph.D. in Autism without giving one single commencement address (which is a shame, really; talk about getting out of graduation in time to beat the lunch crowd – invite a mute to speak. Hearing a pen drop just takes a second) My special-ed high school diploma (which was so special it is not worth the paper it is stamped on) also prepared me well for this advanced degree.

My qualifications are as follows. I'm a contemplative. Before that, I had experience as ADHD, ODD, MR, PDD, ASD, and a BRAT. I am not from the dominant human tribe of neurotypicals. Dominance has a way of creating injustice. The plodding progress of civil rights teaches us that the majority does not respect the rights of the minority until all other options are unpalatable. Please consider this packaged prejudice perspective as you seek, because my lessons always involve justice.

Being a contemplative means I spend most of my time thinking about things that are not present and observing that which is. It is a tidy job, but somebody has to do it. I did not have to be asked twice.

I work hard every day to be my best. My autism does not make it easy, and sometimes I am enraged at having to shoulder this way of being.

Parker Palmer in *To Know as We Are Known* explains it beautifully: "We build a world by the sweat of what lies behind our brows." That is the shingle I am hanging.

So if any of you seek wisdom about autism; slide-on shoes; managing an overprotective mother (aka Smother); the art of pinching, biting and kicking; hiring beefcake personal trainers; or any of my other areas of expertise – please ask.

I am open for business.

Another neurology
B

Addendum – Example of how revolutions build momentum:

After Lois spoke on the news regarding a study correlating autism rates and air pollution, Mule and Muse Productions was bombarded with feedback that was not all flattering – which happens when looking in valuable mirrors. Turns out that unauthorized and unappreciated chin hairs are the least of our worries. We discuss doing better:

Me = My words should be in red.

Lois = I just learned of a study which found men and woman regarded human faces with red backgrounds as more sexy and attractive.

Me = Right, I'll be red. You should be beige.

Lois = That won't show up in print.

Barb = What's your point?

Lois = The irony of playing your straight man is not lost on me.

Barb = The camera adds ten pounds, but it is not supposed to be in hair, unless it is a Nashville production.

Lois = So, with the exception of my over-combed Gene Simmons coiffure, I thought the WBIR interview went well. I was surprised at the backlash from the autism community.

Barb = LOL! You are adorkable. I need to make my point before I get hangry, and Pluto you like a hanging chad. SS, language matters. We the people determine what words get into the dictionary and how they are defined and used. I just watched Anne Curzan's TED talk, "What Makes a Word Real," and added these fresh beauties to my official writing repertoire: "LOL" (Laugh out Loud), "adorkable" (combination of adorable and dork), "hangry" (being cranky or angry as a result of hunger), "Pluto" (demote), and chad (perhaps not as viscerally as Al Gore, but we all learned what a hanging chad was in 2000). Curzan's research fortifies my people's argument that traditional medical language used by psychologists and other "fix-it" specialists pathologizes autism.

Lois = I am getting it. It seems many of the big lessons I learn in life result from my impulsive mistakes. The best I can do is to take more time to thoughtfully consider the perspectives of others. You taught me that. I am hearing logical, heartfelt arguments that "We don't have to call autism a disorder or a disease to acknowledge that Autistic people are disabled and can require accommodations."

Barb = After about five years of working with you, I wrote, "I have done more thinking in each of the past five years than in the previous twenty-nine combined." Sounds like it took a baker's dozen years for your oven light to come on.

Lois = Mute instructions are harder to hear.

Barb = And harder to forget.

Lois = I will give much more consideration to my language, as years of exposure to the status quo in research has clearly bent it to the medical model, which I am understanding may be offensive. I am teachable. I will mindfully practice incorporating fresh terminology, like Ariane Zurcher's definition of autism: "Autism is a type of neurology."

Barb = But wait – there's more…

Lois = And, I shared the following Medical and Social Models chart with the practitioners in our group and posted it prominently in our office.

MEDICAL / SOCIAL MODELS

Medical And Social Model Thinking In Schools

MEDICAL MODEL THINKING	SOCIAL MODEL THINKING
Child is faulty	Child is Valued
Diagnosis	Strengths and Needs defined by self and others
Labeling	Identify Barriers and develop solutions
Impairment becomes Focus of attention	Outcome based programme designed
Assessment, monitoring, programmes of therapy imposed	Resources are made available to Ordinary services
Segregation and alternative services	Training for Parents and Professionals
Ordinary needs put on hold	Relationships nurtured
Reentry if normal enough OR Permanent Exclusion	Diversity Welcomed, Child is Included
Society remains unchanged	Society Evolves

Barb = And while you are wearing that "just another autism expert regurgitating all the usual stuff" hairshirt, don't forget to use my man Nick Walker's definition of autism:

"Autism is a genetically based human neurological variant. The complex set of interrelated characteristics that distinguish autistic neurology from non-autistic neurology is not yet fully understood, but current evidence indicates that the central distinction is that autistic brains are characterized by particularly high levels of synaptic connectivity and responsiveness. This tends to make the autistic individual's subjective experience more intense and chaotic than that of non-autistic individuals; on both the sensorimotor and cognitive levels, the autistic mind tends to register more information, and the impact of each bit of information tends to be both stronger and less predictable."

For more elaboration please see Nick's blog:
http://neurocosmopolitanism.com/what-is-autism/

Lois = Done.

Barb = Nick is right. And you psychologists do not have to abandon science to be of help. Below is what my cutie patootie neurofeedback specialist, Dr. Rex Cannon, just wrote to my family and me (it was my specific request to include my parents) about my brain-map progress. See how Dr. Rexiepoo has nice hair and language. (I am training my brain with neurofeedback so I may be physically more still when I choose, making eye exams and dental work less Michael Jackson risky.) Please show my color brain maps too; folks will appreciate my sexy mind.

Below are Barbs pre EOB and post EOB compared to the database. Due to the volume of movement artifacts I utilized a Laplace montage, which in essence smoothes the signal in order to select the most reliable segments of data for comparison to the database, as well as between conditions. Barb presented with numerous power amplitude and connectivity excesses. This suggests in terms of self regulation her resources are extremely compromised and therefore the degree of energy necessary to perform simple tasks, including being still and monitoring her movements is a difficult task. At the most recent baseline (right) she has reduced a large degree of the amplitude and connectivity excesses across the cortex, however, these may fluctuate relative to internal state or other covert issues we cannot be aware of (eg bodily disturbances). In the relative power maps she has increased alpha power over parietal leads, which is important to the gradual improvement in self-regulation. The goal for the last round of neurofeedback would be to concentrate on the sensory-motor rhythm over the motor cortex, with the goal to aid her in developing more control over her body and movements and allow resources to be freed up for potential learning to occur. Learning may just occur at the motor and sensory level; however, this self-regulation of her bodily movements may have substantial effects across domains. It may also benefit some sense of control and success within her. We will continue to collect baselines at every session to monitor her progress over the next round of sessions.

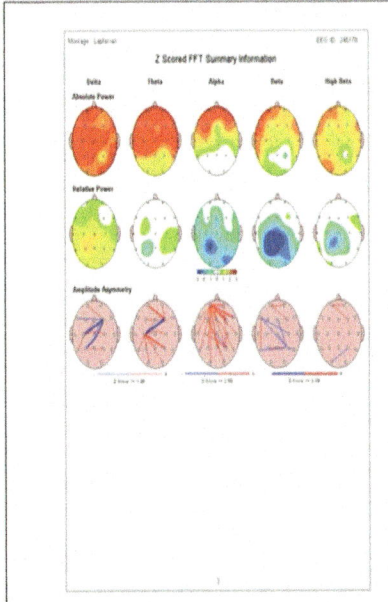
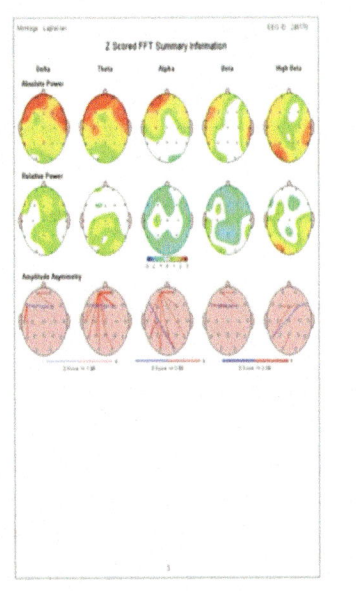

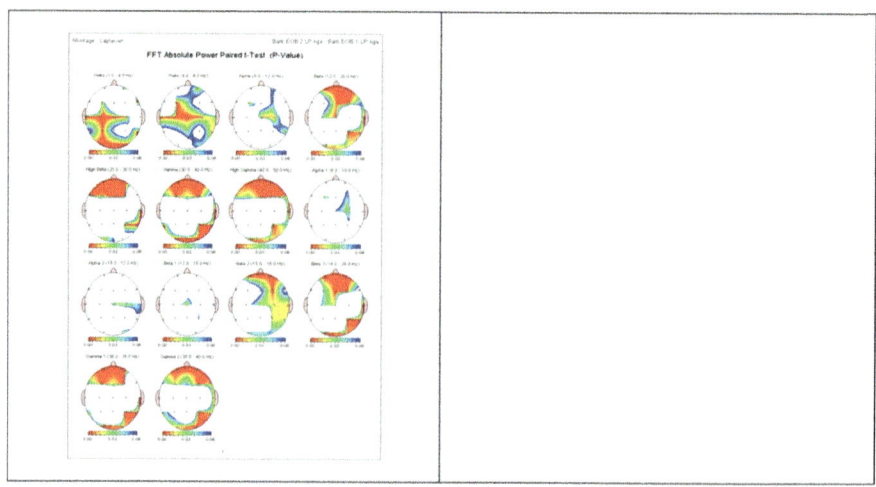

Lois = Learning is always a two-way relationship. Practitioners benefit from the passionate teachings of those we serve, when we are smart enough to listen. On a personal note, I really appreciated your having my back – even when you disagreed with me.

Barb = Actually, what I typed was, "We are all right." Judy Endow's article, "Is Autism a Disability or Difference," puts it well: "So many ideas in the larger autism community often become a debate. As an autistic, this black-or-white, choose-your-side sort of thinking is very neurologically friendly to me. I like clear choices. But I also believe we are often unwittingly duped into believing we need to choose a side only because the idea is presented as a dichotomous choice."

Lois = You don't see it as a dichotomous choice?

Barb = The tree of life has many branches. No need to swing on just one. Enjoy the whole tree. BUT, it is wise to mind your herbicidal cologne and language because that is known to help some limbs thrive.

Lois = Understood. Barb, will you share one of your "momma bear" responses?

Barb = Sure. It will help my "toilet water belongs in the toilet" campaign.

Barb the defender (Barb's response to one of Lois' critics):
Yeah, every autistic person has a brain, as do almost all therapists. My Smiling Shrink's (SS) brain, connected to that all-too-often-open mouth, is not perfect. I read your email, but I did not hear her say "deficit," "pathology," or "suffers from." And it sounds to me like she was not saying that pollutants cause autism, only that there is empirical evidence that suggests we auts are more susceptible to environmental toxins. I may agree with that, as just this week a lady I was interviewing wore cheap perfume – and Hiroshimaed my entire being. I am still shaking some of that sticky bomb out of my cells. I figure if SS can forgive me for biting her until she bleeds, on occasion, or smearing my sh#!t when in her care, I can forgive her for referring to autism as "a disorder," "a disability," and "devastating." You ask, "How can I support this?" Buddy, in the same way Lois supports me: with love, respect, and a hearty dose of presumed competence. As advertised, SS connects with me – and then I share my strengths and interests – and she helps me be who I choose. I hope my take eases your soaring mind and sore heart. I cherish our friendship. All about clearing the air, B

Practical Implications:

1. Courage and connection are needed to give all gifts, and this is our collective purpose.
   It takes both mules and muses to make perceptual changes.
2. If I can have a seat at the table, so can you! The Cool Kids table is now open. It feels like our collective hard work has paid off – and we are now on the right side of history!
   I am asking people to sit with me – and they are.
   This is new to me, and priceless.
   This excerpt from my last book best describes how the table has turned:

"Some skinny coed is repulsed, and reported me to the etiquette authorities. No sh!#t. A teacher comes up to me, and in all seriousness, tells me I am going to have to eat somewhere else because I am making the other children sick.

"God knows I did not wish to stand in the way of the nutritional demands of hundreds of growing normals. The queasy tattletale alone was in danger of a Karen Carpenter-like fate, had one more tomato sandwich (hold the mayo) evaded her lips.

"The normals had allowed me to rub elbows with them for years. But they were finally drawing the line. Who could blame them?"

With your help, this neurodiversity revolution will continue, and you and your children will sit comfortably wherever.
Please pass the sugar... and salt.

Revolutionary B

Eli is only fourteen here but appears to already have children... No wait, that is Ty and me with him in Utah.

Chapter 16
ADHD
by Lois Prislovsky

"You can't stop the waves but you can learn to surf." Jon Kabat-Zinn

One of the reasons Barb and I work so well together is that we balance each other. She is over-stimulated and I am under-stimulated. Research indicates that the brains of individuals with autism show higher-than-normal connectivity or "hyper-connectivity" along many neural networks (*JAMA Psychiatry, June 26, 2013*). And although new research suggests that ADHD is more complicated than just a sluggish Dopamine system, studies show most of us with ADHD have less Dopamine, a neurotransmitter responsible for, among other things, motivation, reward seeking and movement. We therefore are prone to a constant craving for stimulation and motor activity.

In Neurodiversity: Discovering the Extraordinary Gifts of Autism, ADHD, Dyslexia, and Other Brain Differences, Thomas Armstrong explains that in ADHD, "the restraint areas of the brain do not appear to be keeping the emotional and motor areas of the brain in check, resulting in symptoms of hyperactivity and impulsivity." Sometimes that looks like this:

Late one summer afternoon, I had just gotten home from work. Before I could close the kitchen door, Barb and her personal assistant, Tere, entered. Barb lives next door, so this is not uncommon, but she usually makes such unannounced visits solo to steal cheese – handfuls of shredded mild cheddar if she and the beagle are lucky, as it is a messy crime. Tere explained, "Someone is in Barb's house" – they were sure of it. "We definitely heard lots of banging around upstairs." Tere had already called the police, but wanted to wait in our house until the law arrived. Interesting.

I immediately went to check it out. On the walk over to Barb's front door, I saw Tere's truck door open, and there was a ten-inch, serrated hunting knife sheathed in her cup holder. Tere is a nature guide and Barb can get aggressive, so I did not think this sight strange. I helped myself to the knife and entered the house, armed to investigate. It was exciting – I had no idea who or what I would encounter as I searched each room. As only a middle-aged, white woman in a fitted pink blouse, tasteful linen skirt, and matching heels wielding a dagger can do, I "cleared" the house.

I found nothing. I headed out to report my findings. When I opened Barb's front door to exit (still pointing this huge knife in front of me), two police officers greeted me – "greeted" – not met – not confronted – they literally greeted me with smiles, "How may we help you, ma'am?" These officers were not four feet in front of a clearly armed woman, who for all they know could be the maniacal offender, and they did not draw weapons, flinch, or even ask me to put the knife down. Barb had now moved from the kitchen to the side yard – a safe enough distance not to be stabbed or entangled with an intruder but close enough to witness the weird show. The polite professionals "cleared" the house again and found the culprit: several shelves holding plants had collapsed onto each other, and three large houseplants had fallen and broken in stages. On my quest for novel stimulation, I did not register the vacuuming need – because I was looking for criminals and ferocious beasts, not befallen potting soil.

The point is not that I clearly do not look threatening – although that is something I may need to work on – it is that like many with ADHD, I enjoy excitement and often leap before I look. This is a trait, not a disability. Who do you think discovered that lobster is edible? No doubt someone with ADHD: "Hmmm, I'll swim down and get that – menacing pincers – meh, I'll figure something out."

If we treat or medicate away ADHD, we may lose adventurers, explorers, protectors, inventors, athletes and other bold contributors.

Instead, we are wise to embrace and build on the considerable strengths linked with ADHD brain styles. Many of the challenges associated with ADHD can be alleviated with education. Performance may be maximized by understanding the differences, and taking action to establish external and internal structures supporting this type of neurology.

The strength-building approach is growing, and books like *Bright Not Broken: Gifted Kids, ADHD, and Autism* by Diane Kennedy, Rebecca Banks, and Temple Grandin do a good job of shifting the focus away from deficits.

Lynn Weiss, author of *Attention Deficit Disorder in Adults: A Different Way of Thinking,* shares this list of "Twenty-nine positive attributes of ADD" (a term she uses to include both ADD and ADHD):

1. Sensitive
2. Empathetic with the feelings of others
3. Feels things deeply
4. Creative in nature (including problem solving)
5. Inventive
6. Often sees things from a unique perspective
7. Great at finding things that are lost
8. Perceptually acute
9. Stand-up comic
10. Spontaneous
11. Fun
12. Energetic
13. Open and un-secretive
14. Eager for acceptance and willing to work for it
15. Responsive to positive reinforcement
16. Doesn't harbor resentment
17. Quick to do what one likes to do
18. Difficult to fool
19. Looks past surface appearance to the core of people, situations, and issues
20. Down to earth
21. Good networker
22. Sees unique relationships between people and things
23. Cross-disciplinary and interdisciplinary
24. Less likely to get in a rut or go stale
25. Original with a sense of humor
26. Observant
27. Loyal

28. Intense when interested in something
29. More likely to do things because they want to than because they should, thus wholehearted in efforts.
[30. Flexible about folks not identifying one more positive attribute to make it an even thirty.]

Below are some Do's and Don'ts that may help structure a life well suited for maximizing ADHD strengths. (They are written from the perspective of parenting a child with ADHD, but are also applicable for self-care.)

Do:

1. Do know your medications. While I recommend doing comprehensive lifestyle and educational support first to eliminate or reduce the need for medications, many people find medication helpful. The two main chemicals to enhance attention are Methylphenidate (e.g., Ritalin, Concerta, Focalin, and Daytrana) and Dextroamphetamine (e.g., Dexedrine, Adderall, Vyvanse, ProCentra). Understand the time-release mechanisms associated with your child's prescription, and teach it to them in straightforward terms that they can comprehend. When they are more educated about the drug's half-life, effectiveness, and side effects, they are likely to take more responsibility for taking their meds, and to increase their mindfulness about how it influences their mood and behavior. This knowledge is empowering, and they become better patients and self-advocates.
2. Do understand the benefits of a diet tailored to enhance cognitive processing and minimize ADHD challenges. What is good for the brain is good for ADHD. Empirical research supports the following dietary suggestions:
   a) High-protein diet (beans, cheese, eggs, meat, milk, and nuts)
   b) Few simple carbohydrates (sparingly consume things like white flour and rice, candy, and sugary drinks.) Eliminate simple sugars whenever possible.

c) Lots of complex carbohydrates and whole grains, along with legumes and vegetables, which gradually supply the glucose necessary for the brain to function without the rapid insulin response.

d) More Omega-3 fatty acids like those found in cold-water fish, walnuts, Brazil nuts, and olive and canola oil. Small, frequent meals are the most beneficial to keep blood-sugar levels and mood stabilized, and even increase the length of time that ADHD medications work. A daily 100% vitamin and mineral substitute is also recommended. Nutrition matters.

3. Do structure at least thirty minutes each day of sustained cardiovascular exercise for your child. Daily exercise is perhaps the most effective treatment for ADHD in terms of reducing negative symptoms and the need for or amount of medications. In addition to improving circulation and thus mental sharpness, exercise provides additional opportunities for socialization and navigating novel environments, which promote neuronal health. Norman Doidge, the author of *The Brain That Changes Itself: Stories of Personal Triumph from the Frontiers of Brain Science*, writes: "Nothing speeds brain atrophy more than being immobilized in the same environment: the monotony undermines our dopamine and attentional systems crucial to maintaining brain plasticity."

4. Do make sleep hygiene a priority. Sleep is vital for healthy brain growth and regulation. The ability to sustain alertness is dependent on it. Have a set bedtime ritual and time and stick to it. Keep it positive; make the ritual be quiet quality time with your child. Scratching your child's back while telling them a story, "out of your mouth," is one bedtime ritual my child has enjoyed for all his fifteen years. Find out what type of attentive, tender connection works best for your child – and make it a mutually enjoyable tradition.

5. Do help your child understand and build on his/her strengths. Discuss openly with your child as his/her ability to process vocabulary and scientific processes grows. Share that individuals with ADHD have less Dopamine than most people. Explain that

Dopamine is a chemical in the brain associated with movement, motivation, and reward seeking. Because of this, people with ADHD often seek movement, lots of stimulation, and even thrills. This is not a bad way to be – just different. Such distinct talents often produce outstanding entrepreneurs, athletes, explorers, etc. **Finding out where individuals with ADHD feel most competent and at ease provides good footing for connection.** Instead of asking people to do what they can't, renowned neuroscientist and prolific brain-research expert, Michael Merzenich, teaches us that the best way to improve thinking is **building on abilities – and this is the best path to strengthen weaknesses.**

Don't:

1. Don't focus on deficits. There is no gold-standard brain, just as there is no standard flower, culture, or race. Diversity of brains, like biodiversity, is by design. Individuals with ADHD do have brains wired differently than most, and no one disputes the inefficiency of this particular design for performing activities like sitting still and paying attention to low-reward activities. But there are two sides of this neurological coin. The flip side is that those with ADHD are often adventurous, have a keen perception of the whole picture, are drawn to abstract ideas, possess remarkable intuition, and have lots of energy. For best results, positively reinforce their strengths and create an environment that embraces diversity. **Work hard to let your children know that human excellence comes in all packages – so they are invited to be themselves.**

2. Don't permit unlimited access to video games. Due to decreased Dopamine, children with ADHD often crave video games that offer players intense action, constant and immediate rewards, competition, and thrilling stories that are rare in everyday life. Such gaming does not help your child build social skills, postponed gratification, and physical exercise – all of which are known to help reduce the negative aspects of ADHD. Consistent boundaries should be set regarding the amount and type of video

gaming that can be played each day. Those requiring gross motor movements such as X-box Connect, and Wii activities like sports, dance, music, and fitness games, are preferable to the more sedentary, hand-held-controller games. Significant research shows that children with ADHD learn more and are happier when involved in intense physical activity (preferably outdoors and while being social), so limiting video game time to no more than one hour per day is recommended. Positive reinforcement is best for shaping and sustaining behavior, so parents may wish to use this as the carrot cake to be enjoyed after homework and other responsibilities are accomplished.

3. Don't make unrealistic restrictions on movement. Those with ADHD think best when moving. Whenever possible, incorporate movement with learning. Your child may enjoy swinging or going on a walk with you while reading aloud or silently. Reading and discussing homework with you while they are on a stationary bike, treadmill, or Pilates ball works, too. Another suggestion is to toss a ball back and forth as you and your child do a question-and-answer exchange while reviewing for tests. Make sure your child asks you questions on the material too. It is empowering, and it helps them process the material in multiple ways.

4. Don't lower expectations for your child in reaching their potential through hard work and goal-oriented progressions. Help them to understand that ADHD is a different way of processing that comes with challenges – and many advantages. With diet, exercise, good sleep habits, and mindfulness, medications can be reduced if not eliminated. Side effects of ADHD drugs (decreased appetite, insomnia, headaches, etc.) are dose-dependent, so encourage your children to develop coping strategies built on their strengths to accomplish their goals and dreams. As your child learns more about how he/she learns, he/she will become empowered, and self-control, confidence, and responsibility will increase.

5. Don't take yourself too seriously, so that you may connect easily with your child and help him/her lighten up about mistakes, thereby providing courage to try their best. The following is an

excerpt from our book *I Might Be You* to provide an example of such relationship-building exchanges.

An accepting and playful tone encourages others to take the risk and effort to connect with us by reducing the fear of "not getting it right." A client of mine, M.N., a nine-year-old boy with social anxiety, dyslexia, and ADHD, asked me, "What was the stupidest thing you have ever done?" Never wanting to miss a teaching/connecting opportunity, my wheels spun as I sifted through my mental repertoire of stupid things. A bit surprised about the bulk of that category, I mentally moved on to an age and clinically appropriate category themed, "Seemed Like a Good Idea at the Time." I shared that when I was about his age, my best pals Steve and Brian and I were setting booby traps in our fort. My innovative contribution was to balance a fireplace log atop the door, so that when an intruder dared to open it… *Wham!* Log drop on the head (decades before the movie *Home Alone*, I might add). As one with intact frontal lobes may imagine, little Lois soon became distracted with other play tasks and forgot all about the log, so – Wham! Log drop on head. I came to quickly, and we resumed play. Later, in the heat of stick-gun army maneuvers around the Walkers' house, Steve said, "Hey Weezie (we all had nicknames, some more reasonable than others), didn't you have on a white shirt?" Indeed. Nothing bleeds like the noggin. My shirt was crimson. Mom, a stoic RN who knew how to stretch a dollar, soaked the shirt and mended my scalp. My cautionary tale took maybe a minute and fifteen seconds of his session. In that time, M.N.:

1. practiced being physically still and attentive
2. related we are all works in progress
3. observed that it is possible to lighten up about mistakes
4. learned that nothing bleeds like the head and
5. maybe, just maybe, put together that it is wise to pay extra attention – especially when something seems like a good idea at the time.

Below are suggestions for older teens and adults with ADHD:

1. If you only adopt one recommendation – pick EXERCISE! Exercise vigorously and regularly. Understand that you are drawn to intense stimuli, and go for it. Plan guilt-free excitement outlets. A little planning goes a long way here, trust me. Making arrangements to try kite surfing or go mountain biking on a new expert course you have no business being on sure beats (hypothetically speaking) scrambling to find buddies with bail money in the middle of the night after you spontaneously decided to climb the bell tower.

2. For those of us with ADHD brain styles, structure is critically important for balance and well-being. For example, to foster more reliable attention, I go to sleep and wake up at basically the same time every day – even on vacation. External structure like this helps to pattern planning for efficient thinking and performance. Having a plan establishes a thoughtfully balanced life. I recommend scheduling everything you can: work, exercise, eating, sex, sleep, quality time with your children, quality time with your spouse, quality time with yourself, and quality time with _____ (you know who needs to be in this space for you). **Designating a time for everything may allow you to better focus on one connection at a time**. This type of mindful focus on who or what is in front of you adds to the quality of your relationships and productivity. Last night at dinner, my fifteen-year old son said, "Mom, a few weeks ago you asked me who is the most easy for me to talk with, in terms of who best fits with my humor, tone, sensitivities, logic, speed, and conversational cadence – you know – whom do I get to talk to without making any adjustments to myself. Remember, I told you I needed to think about it. I did. And it is you." I teared up with gratitude, as I know that precious few parents get to converse with their children without the slightest hint of awkwardness. I know he will use this knowledge and experience to build many comfortable and rewarding relationships. If we can achieve this level of connection, so can you and yours. It just takes practicing your focused intention to be precisely who the other

person needs you to be at that moment. Now that we are on the topic of putting the other person first, let's transition to Tip 3, which is less warm and fuzzy (or not – depending on your tastes).

3. Let the other person come first... literally.

Best-selling author Brene Brown explains, "Compassion is not a relationship between the healer and the wounded. It's a relationship between equals. Compassion becomes real when we recognize our shared humanity. And we share with people who earn the right to hear the story." One of the "come passion" stories I have been entrusted with over the years is that it often works best when the person with ADHD makes sure his/her partner has an orgasm first. It seems all that excitement, energy and movement makes for fantastic sex until the ADHD person is no longer motivated, and therefore loses interest and focus. It is like that classic neuropsychology experiment, where the hunger area of the lateral hypothalamus is lesioned by an electrode attached directly into the brain of the laboratory rat. The rat is immediately no longer interested in food – in fact, if it's eating, the food pellet drops out of its mouth. (If Barb can write about smearing feces being part of her autism, I can share ADHD sex-life hacks. My wife, who is a little more concerned about our sex-life reputation than I, would like me to add that sometimes we come together... but honestly that is rare, and this book is about practical advice, not lassoing leap-year unicorns.)

4. Be patient with yourself as you learn more and do better. As Deepak Chopra reminds us in *Super Brain: Unleashing the Explosive Power of Your Mind to Maximize Health, Happiness, and Spiritual Well-Being*: "You are not your brain. Perception isn't passive. You are not simply receiving a fixed, given reality. You are shaping it. Self-awareness changes perception." The key is to keep moving forward or, as Barb types,

> "I find patience to be rather like a marathon, and similarly exciting in the sense that it is a testament to human endurance and perseverance. One sips water along the way, eats a few bananas – letting the mind wander to other

matters but never losing sight of the goal or the sustained effort it takes to achieve it. As in aging, the trick is to maintain grace and not lose bowel control."

5. We know that what we focus on grows. Make a habit of taking a moment to focus your intention clearly. As I shared in our last book, *I Might be You: An Exploration of Autism and Connection,* I recommend taking a moment to focus your intention on the best interest of the other(s) before every session, meeting, class, practice, operation... or whatever form your day takes.

Generous intentions connect us – and connection is the point of living.

When you have a better understanding of the other person's brain style, it is easier to help. Below is an actual session note for an eleven-year-old girl who was able to use her strengths to find her solutions.

8-5-2015 = Today I.J., her mom and I discussed her tics as an impulsivity issue. These are common in about 25% of children, and they are typically seen to progress from the face or eyes southward down the body. It is likely that I.J. is under-stimulated and has the impulse to twitch or move to help her stay engaged. She clearly thinks best when moving. So we collaborated on an approach to have I.J. replace the socially awkward tic with a less-noticeable movement – but one that would also bring her release when the pressure builds up. I.J. chose a toe curl and release. We talked about habit-reversal therapy and called it "twitch switch," which I.J. clearly understood immediately. She got that the most important part of twitch switch is the application of a competing response whenever she notices a tic or urge to tic. We then did a hypnosis exercise, designed to help her monitor her relaxation and control her focus. I.J. gave us feedback on her experience today and said, "I think it may take about two weeks to make the switch." I think she may be right – especially if I.J. begins to practice the switch both consciously and unconsciously.

As Edward Hallowell, author of *Driven to Distraction: Recognizing and Coping with Attention Deficit Disorder from*

Childhood through Adulthood, says: "Fear and shame are the only true disabilities." I encourage you to structure your life to best support your natural style of brain construction – and then live your life with gusto.

After my public blog exchange with Dr. Andrew Solomon, he graciously agreed to be one of my first guests on Loud Mute Radio. He is a class act in every way. This dashing duo is Andrew (right) and his husband John. You know you look good when you make Van Dyck's models appear underdressed. In the conversation B

Chapter 17
Don't Believe Everything You Think: A Review
by Barb Rentenbach

"Our children don't have to display musical genius to forever change the way that we hear it. They don't have to create museum-worthy art to make art-worthy art. They don't have to choreograph like Balanchine to make us understand that dance is language. Autistics don't have to be prodigies to find value in their everyday skills and to use those skills to compensate for their challenges. They don't have to be savants to live lives that matter and that make the world a better place for all of us. They just need to have the chance to try." Jess Wilson

Now that I know my purpose is to write, my world-view has expanded. Like all writers, I read, and I research, what interests me. Turns out there are many of us who are tasked to allocate different perceptions. Daniel Tammet, author of *Born on a Blue Day*, teaches that personal perceptions are how we all come to know what we know. The more perceptions we can process, the more reality we may know.

Stephen Hawking, whose physicality makes my odd moves look Sasha Cohen smooth, writes in *The Grand Design,* "A few years ago, the city council of Monza, Italy, barred pet owners from keeping goldfish in curved goldfish bowls. The measure's sponsor explained the measure in part by saying that it is cruel to keep a fish in a bowl with curved sides because, gazing out, the fish would have a distorted view of reality. But how do we know we have the true, undistorted picture of reality? Might not we ourselves also be inside some big goldfish bowl and have our vision distorted by an enormous lens? The goldfish's picture of reality is different from ours, but can we be sure it is less real?"

In this chapter, I share my world-view exchange with one of the greatest thinkers and dressers of our time, Dr. Andrew Solomon.

REDUNDANCY WARNING: My dear style editor, herself neurodiverse (ADHD & bisexual) and mother to neurodiverse children (ADHD and Asperger's), urged me to cut the redundant pieces in this chapter so as not to insult reader intelligence. Believe me, I know the infuriating feel of patronization when someone repeats information. Before you become offended, please know that this chapter is designed as folk art. The handmade quilts I see in the South are warm blankets of padding, enclosed between recycled bits of fabric, kept in place by lines of stitching. Typing is the fabric of my life. I can't sew, or even wipe my own ass, but I made this word quilt. Please skip if it angers you; otherwise, I hope you enjoy the warmth and beauty of my design.

Open-Hearted Letter Quilt to Andrew Solomon
by Barb Rentenbach

Dear Andrew,

My buddy Jess Wilson, of "Diary of a Mom" fame, asked my non-verbal Autistic self to weigh in on your latest controversy.

As my tattletale thighs attest, I weigh plenty, and I am happy to share myself fully – as I believe that is precisely what is missing.

It's like Saxe's (1873) poem, "The Blind Men and the Elephant," where each blind man is partly in the right as he describes a portion of an elephant he studies, but all are in the wrong in knowing an elephant.

This autistic pachyderm will expand perceptions by presenting more pieces.

Being from Tennessee, I think perhaps a quilt is the best way to show another neurology position pieced together from myself – much of which I retrieved from the scrap pile, as others often devalued my strange bits. Handmade quilts take a long time, and that is part of their value. I type one painstaking letter at a time, sewing my words carefully and preserving them for future use. Like me, this gift is made from new and old pieces. May it blanket as a warm polemic.

In your March 17th, 2014 *New Yorker* article, "The Reckoning," about the Sandy Hook killer, you wrote, "Both autism and psychopathology entail a lack of empathy. Psychologists, though, distinguish between the 'cognitive empathy' deficits of autism (difficulty understanding what emotions are, trouble interpreting other people's non-verbal signs) and the 'emotional empathy' deficits of psychopathy (lack of concern about hurting other people, an inability to share their feelings)."

I will comment on that one paragraph. Your other fifty-five paragraphs I found to be provocative and factual, and I was delighted to harvest a new word: "sclerotic." I am a collector. Thanks! (BTW, fifty-six paragraphs = twenty-eight victims times two controversies. Patterns were my first love.)

Cognitive empathy deficits are not part of my untidy truth. However, it is what you know to be true because it is what you dutifully researched from what is known in science at this time.

In 1968, this same science depicted homosexuality as a psychiatric disorder: *This category is for individuals whose sexual interests are directed primarily toward objects other than people of the opposite sex..." (Page 44 from DSM II)*

This *mental disorder* diagnosis of *Sexual Deviation-Homosexuality (302.0)* allowed mental-health providers to bill insurance *and* perform "reparative therapy," which is treatment to change a person from a homosexual or bisexual orientation to a "normal" or heterosexual orientation.)

In 1974, homosexuality was removed from the list of mental illnesses. Scientific breakthrough? Nope. Gay people kicked up a fuss.

Let the ASD quilting bee begin.

If you want to know more about Autism Spectrum Disorder (ASD), ask a person with ASD. But, that logic actually brings us to another controversy. Is it possible for people with severe ASD to communicate logically? Many think not.

The truth is many, like myself, think well.

Autism is my prism, not my prison. I will stitch till my lifeline-typing finger is crippled with overuse to share my reality of intelligence and cognitive empathy.

Justice almost always takes more time than the just expect it to.

Luckily for us, patience is often an ASD strength. What normals perceive as "waiting" and "wasting time," we may view as stasis. Like well-seasoned Tibetan monks, we are in no rush. We understand the reality of impermanence. We understand the reality that nothing is as it appears to be. Please, consider here my hypothesis that there are more autistics now because of human evolution. Autism may serve to provide the individual time and space to contemplate and meditate more so than any convent or monastery. Nonverbals "waste no time" on vows of silence. We simply live it.

Please give our humanity the benefit of the doubt.

After years of toiling with all I am, I can now type, with just one hand touching my back for support, to help me initiate movement and overcome my apraxia. The National Institute of Health defines apraxia (called dyspraxia if mild) as a neurological disorder characterized by loss of the ability to execute or carry out learned movements despite having the desire and ability to perform them. This includes talking and typing. I also struggle with ataxia, which is characterized by imbalance, unsteady walk and tendency to stumble, problems with fine-motor movements, and difficulty positioning in space. I often politely ask my brain to please move my hand to do this or that, only to be told, "We're sorry, due to high autism volume, we are not able to answer your call at this time. Please try harder later."

Andrew, this is the second time I have written about an ASD controversy you sparked. I admire luminous incendiaries like yourself. You are vital for the evolution of humanity. We autistics are fully human and intend to be a part of such solutions. Our humanity is too often veiled by blind men who do not see our intelligence and sentience. This quilt has two sides.

Side One: Intelligence

I have been fighting this specific misperception all my life. Andrew, I don't look normal. I appear quite messed up, and a prime candidate for nothing but pity and patronization, with a sprinkling of repulsion and fear. I am disguised as a poor thinker.

Like many others with ASD, I think well, but as my friend and harbinger of ASD truths Emma Zurcher Long types, *"Language is an awkward way to communicate." I argue that this is true for everyone, but highly challenging for those of us who are autistically wired. It took me years to think in language. But prior to that, my thinking was not faulty: it was just not language-based. Thinking in language is not efficient for me. I wish I could give you a pretty little fact package about what works, so that folks like me could get such opportunities and soar socially and academically. Of course, the problem is… it is hard to say in language. Typing makes it way easier, because I can control the speed of each thought and break it down into smaller parts, to be better described by letters one peck at a time. Speaking requires a rather unnatural process for me – perhaps like you singing a song you heard in another language. You may be able to imitate the sounds, but the meaning in each mimic is not precise. The best way for me now is to communicate through typing. But still, my thinking is not easily translated into words. Feelings, sensations, visions and knowings that are cleanly processed in my mind don't fit well into letter symbols. There, I said it – or something close.*

In Western culture, significant people live outside of their minds. Just as the homeless are at a disadvantage because they must directly weather storms, cold, heat, and myriad dangers, those of us who exist invisibly in the conscious dream country of our minds suffer similar prejudices, because we hardly exist in the external world and are therefore not censused.

The **bold italic** content below is from my August 7th, 2013 blog about your first ASD controversy, where readers considered whether the world was better off with or without autism.

What inspired me to do this giveaway of my audiobook – I Might Be You: An Exploration of Autism and Connection – was the recent controversy concerning the autism chapter in Andrew Solomon's artfully researched bestseller, Far From the Tree. (The book took him ten years to write. I can relate to that type of perseverance, even though I suspect Andrew may type with all ten well-manicured fingers, and not just one autistically wired, nail-bitten digit, like me, but who am I to judge if he needs extra time.) Many in our autistic

149

community wish to boycott his book, as they find it to be filled with harmful parenting horror stories. I wrote on that below, and have since heard the chapter. We non-verbal auts often enjoy learning with audiobooks, as we can usually do so under our own steam. Which is why this giveaway is audiobook specific.

Solomon is a master storyteller. He relays tales of parents in harrowing, sustained pain. He gifts these real people a voice. These overwhelmed parents are being heard.

Below is my comment following Jessica Wilson's "Diary of a Mom" account of this controversy. The next comment comes from a special-education counselor (The kind of "special" that nobody, I mean NOBODY, wants to be). See Dick run about his trouble with hardness.

Barb comments,

"it is true autism is hard. i have autism, the hard kind. but i have decided to be up to the challenge as my parents did because there is no other palatable option. andrew solomon is no enemy of those of us who are here with jess to "demystify the condition and to humanize the people behind the label in the public eye" because andrew is genuinely trying to know. so should we. andrew will learn from us and we from him. life is perspective. to live a balanced wholehearted life we are wise to learn how we are perceived so we may better connect with others and each respect who we chose to be. so, i just purchased "far from the tree" to learn more of those perspectives knowing they may be hard to hear. i hope andrew will repay my respect and purchase my audiobook, "i might be you: an exploration of autism and connection" so he may learn my hard truths. may we all transform "years of accumulated slights" to the now of empathy and compassion. sometimes hard to hear but listening b

Dick replies: July 12, 2013 at 10:22 pm I'm skeptical that anyone can honestly write "i have autism, the hard kind." I am a 50 y.o. rehabilitation counselor and I work with adults and kids with autism – the hard kind – every day. None can read. None can write. None even know what autism is. THAT is "the hard kind." I also work with adults and kids that have autism – the not-so-hard kind – who read and write and drive. But people who have "the hard kind" of autism can't write about it. They can't even talk about it.

Barb comments back to Dick: July 15, 2013 at 10:50 am dear dick, it is my hope you will be open to knowing that many of us who are disguised as poor thinkers are, in fact, more like you than you may choose to believe. we may have a variety of physical and mental challenges, confounded by profound difficulties with communication, which shroud our humanity. i invite you to please take a few moments to read this link about how some of us with the hard kind have broken through with lots of hard work and sustained focus. thank you for caring. real b "a note on how this book was written" http://muleandmuseproductions.com/about-the-book-i-might-be-you/

I wrote the measured response to Dick above because I am learning that we all do better when we know better. From my hard, front-row seat to autism, rehabilitation counseling, and special education, I learned that believing one's students are mentally deficient and not capable of sentient thought – much less writing – leads to not teaching Dick. (Oh, did I leave out a comma? If only I could learn to write....)

Almost 100 percent of my teachers thought that way and treated me accordingly – as a lesser being. It only took one teacher who taught from her heart to my heart to change my reality and course. Andrea Reynolds assumed my value and competence. Then so did I. Others followed suit. Today, I choose to no longer allow myself to be excluded from humanity by such perceptions I do not share.

(END previous blog excerpt)

Andrew, I am not alone. Many of us with ASD are happy to teach. (This old dog is all about learning new tricks) To quote my mentor Emma Zurcher Long, who is twelve years old, writing the following by saying each letter aloud that she pointed to on a stencil board: "Autism is not what parents want to hear, but I hope that will change as more people get to know someone like me."

We are all teachers. My style may sometimes be more ribald than others (a gal must take her fun where she can get it) but our message is consistent: It is in our best interest to remember that we are all the same. People are flecks of God. Each God fragment, dispersed through space-time, has a slightly different shape. One shape is not superior to another. All are necessary to complete the perfect, infinite God puzzle. To be proud that one "tolerates" diversity is ludicrous. The whole system is the sum of its parts. Be your part. Connect with other parts, and the God puzzle is revealed.

Andrew, your book, *Far from the Tree*, laid bare the question of whether or not the world is better off with or without autism.

I know that it is better with.

I think autism is a valuable part of human evolution.

Consider the stagnation of our predecessors. *Homo erectus,* who existed for over a million years with basically only axe-like tools, hunting, and the use of fire. No significant technological, ritual, or symbolic improvements were made until *Homo sapiens* appeared, about one hundred thousand years ago. *Homo sapiens* had something *Homo erectus* did not: language, with grammatical, articulate, and referential speech. Language changed the world.

Modern humans became the sole survivor of a complex family tree because language allowed for consciousness of our pasts, our futures, and ourselves. Innovations promoting surviving and thriving exploded. "Life can only be understood backwards, but it must be lived forwards," wrote Soren Kierkegaard.

These days, no human is equipped to process all the sensory and intellectual information available. Information overload is prevalent. Maybe autism is an "evolutionary variation kite," flown to see if such a human-wiring tweak will better equip us to deal with and process infinite information.

Research confirms that documented cases of autism and related spectrum disorders are increasing at unprecedented rates. Autistic tendencies may enable some humans to better weed out time perceptions and social/emotional/external distractions, which may hamper observations needed for specific problem solving. How often do normals take the time to really touch, smell, taste, hear, and truly observe a seemingly common object or parcel of nature?

The American Psychiatric Association's Diagnostic and Statistical Manual, Fifth Edition (DSM-5), lists among the criteria for ASD: deficits in social-emotional reciprocity; deficits in non-verbal communicative behaviors; and deficits in developing, maintaining, and understanding relationships.

I contend, many times, autistics revert to isolation by default rather than preference. It is infinitely easier to back away and not try to be included instead of oafishly stepping in and attempting to convey your intent to be a part.

Loneliness is the most predominant side effect of our unique design. Allow me to try to express the magnitude of isolation in people with brains like mine. The bad news is that the beginning, formative years comprise the most mind-exploding confusion and world abandonment that I think a being can physically withstand. We are talking threshold-of- ceasing-to-exist, because the internal desire to get off this ride is so intense. It is fortunate that most suicide methods take considerable coordination and effort; otherwise autistics would be extinct way before genetic engineering becomes popular. Apparently, wishing to die with more repetition than grains of sand does not always do the trick.

I survived, but did not thrive, until decades later when I eventually found purpose – and true friendships – through words.

It started six years ago, when I gained acceptance from not one, but two neurotypical cohorts. They are not damaged goods, either. Each, about my age, is physically attractive, very educated, and delightful. The purity is that these two buddies connect with me under our own steam. **Obligation fuels no part of our bond.** They are not paid, or service providers for me in any way, or tied to my family. Our only roles are to enjoy each other and have each other's back. (Evolutionarily most beneficial.)

How did this happen? Here is my best guess.

They read my work.

I wrote, "Evolution has not wired all of us to attain such relationships easily. Some humans do not give much thought to having friends – it just happens naturally. One top-heavy toddler hugs the tiny neck of another. From there, they battle with sharing and acquire language and exchange it as a limitless commodity."

Like cheap oil in Dubai, words fuel friendships, and that vital product is taken for granted by the indigenous. Not being from the land of cheap words, Autistics have a very hard time making nonpaid friends. But I finally did it at age thirty-six by getting words (and lots of them) out there. Then, two beings were able to relate to me in a new way.

My slick words were expensive and time consuming to excavate. It is hard to find good help in dystopia, but I did. SS (my Smiling Shrink) helped me drill down and find my crude words. The refinement process took years.

Eventually, my product was ready for market. In *Synergy* and other publications, I shared my past, humor, dreams, flaws, and interests. The same stuff you normals do on your first "friend date." Jessica liked what she read, and contacted me for a chat. After a few email correspondences, I was able to establish my footing. I began to understand that she was not seeking something from me – but seeking me. It took time to acclimate. I was incredulous at first. Jessica was a Ph.D. student in educational psychology – the same field as SS. I fished, but reeled in no evidence that she wanted to study or treat me. Curious. Surely this gal had many good friends. And Jessica is simply not the gold-digger type. I can divine that vein a mile away. What did she want? Should I open the door? After eliminating a series of possible motives, I calculated that the worst-case scenario was that she is another cloyingly pious God Squad activist who believes Hell does not discriminate against mute autistics and is making sure no salvation rock has been left unturned. I did not allow myself to entertain a best-case scenario. So, fortified with my most powerful religious arguments, I met Jessica at SS's office for a face-to-face, so that I could communicate with supported typing.

We had a riveting conversation. Turns out religion was a topic, but that may have been more my doing, since I was prepared to spar. We met like this a couple of times. Jessica never did give me a *Watchtower* pamphlet, instruct me on how to accept Jesus into my heart, or ask for a donation. We simply began to share aspects of our lives, along with plenty of good food, wine, and music. "Simply" is an interesting word choice for something that took thirty-six years to happen.

After I answered the door for Jessica, Elizabeth came a-knocking. She also visits with no agenda other than mutual interests, affinity, and, dare I say it... friendship. A girl could get used to this – and I have. Another friendship followed this one, and I see no end in sight as my welcome mat is out. Words, don't fail me now.

My point is that the DSM-5 describes aspects of me: "Failure of normal back-and-forth conversation, reduced sharing of interests, emotions or affect, abnormalities in eye contact and body language, lack of understanding of the use of gestures, facial expressions and non-verbal communication and absence of interests in peers." But science does this without comprehending that this elephant understands the tea party and may wish to attend – but navigating the play house is DIFFICULT.

Perhaps prevalent autistic characteristics, such as "language problems," may be the precursors to other forms of valid, consistent human communication, which are faster, and more efficient and honest, than speech. Please consider that before language became dominant, surely a minority of humans hard-wired for verbal speech existed and were probably also viewed as "different." Skull remains reveal that these individuals who became known as *Homo sapiens* even looked different, as their face was flatter, which allowed for articulate speech. These are a couple of the many reasons why I have great reservations about genetic engineering and cloning.

The system of heredity depends on variation. Neurodiversity is more than good – it's God. History has shown that when we start trying to eliminate diversity, nature answers cruelly. Take, for example, the self-important European royals who inbred to keep the royal blood pure. How many short-lived, retarded hemophiliacs with big ears (kidding) did that produce?

Can one imagine a world where humility was bred out? Consider who would clone. It would be those same white folks who now spend thousands of dollars each year on infertility treatments, just so little Johnny will be like them. Meanwhile, tiny, beautiful babies of color and with special needs can't get adopted – literally to save their life. My own incredibly smart and supportive mom would have probably chosen the cloning option, if given the choice of that or having a special-needs daughter destined to take a lifetime of care and countless resources. Imagine – she could play golf with a younger version of herself. Heaven, until Mom pulled every muscle trying to compete. See – cloning can even result in severe muscle strain.

Normals are often pleased with themselves, and think they have a good handle on the past and a sound plan for the future, all the while participating with frenzy in the present. My own SS schedules people, places, events, work, leisure, and even passion in endless back-to-back "time" chunks. Her mind incessantly prioritizes these responsibilities and happenings based on a scale made up by normals. She hurries through or skips countless meals and other life joys in order to accomplish. I, on the other hand, have a lovely lunch every day, followed by a relaxing swim or a fulfilling amount of peaceful chill time. I focus on one life concept at a time. For example, this word quilt has been my primary contemplation for close to a month. I am not designed for physical or mental juggling. The outer world seems to value harrowing juggling acts. This autistic has a different perspective. Who is happier and closer to God: a napping native with a warm sun, clean ocean, and plenty of tasty trout, or a chainsaw juggler in a business suit with a buzzing cell phone?

I encourage all to discover your own shape, connect with others, and enjoy your lunch. The result will be resplendent and quite worth doing.

Side two: Sentience

Andrew, you defined cognitive empathy as deficits of autism that involve difficulty understanding what emotions are, and trouble interpreting other people's nonverbal signs. Please know that my cognitive empathy lets me know that you intended no insult – so none was taken.

To show off a little more of my cognitive empathy, please enjoy this excerpt from my previous book.

(Begin excerpt):

For the most part, the life I have chosen is manifesting at the rate I choose. Patience is a virtue, but for me it is more like a third arm. I was born with it – most are not. I wield it to help me juggle emotions, creativity, goals, personal interactions, and mindfulness. My boyfriend Jerry has a third arm, too, but Asperger's is the only diagnosis most would give him. Third arms are not transparent. All can see them if they wish, but most do not because they are not expecting to see them.

I am designed well for my purpose, because my third arm and high pain threshold make me well equipped to harvest justice, as farming it is a slow, painful process. SS was assisting my research on positive and negative liberty, for background material for this piece, when her wife, Ty, came in crying and asked if we could put our work on hold for a few minutes while she got something off her chest. Now, Ty is a formidable woman. She is ex-military, a triathlete, full-time anesthesiologist, resolute friend to me, and a rock in our community. She is no crybaby. As one might imagine, I am a fantastic listener – much better than SS despite her pro status, because she is always strategizing ways to treat and fix. I literally just listen.

Ty tearfully read an article posted on Facebook by one of her business partners presenting "another position to consider" concerning President Obama's statement supporting the right for same-sex couples to marry. The author was dismissive of such families and used crude terms to describe those sex lives. Truth be told, it was titillating, but so much is to the sexually parched. Plus, such acts did not seem exclusive to homosexual couples – but I digress. He went on to accuse Obama of reverse evolution because the President's decision was based in part on how his young daughters perceive families with gay parents as equal. The writer judged divining wisdom from children as ignorant.

I understand why Ty's feelings were hurt. Belittling the validity of her family is mean. I expect if Jerry and I marry, our family will also be put in some pile other than the IN Box with full rights under the law.

It boils down to justice. For now, we nontypicals must suffer at the hands of inconsiderate masses, because the majority does not grant minority equal rights until all other alternatives are shown to be unpalatable.

So, day after day, I write the bitter truth. Each person who truly hears will find the status quo a little harder to swallow.

Like Ty's kind, my ASD clan needs access to government. I was skipped over for a free and appropriate public education because, even though supported typing was allowed for me, an imprimatur was never given permitting my supported typing to count. I moved on, and I now make my own education count.

This planting season, I am focused on harvesting my legal rights as a sentient adult. As it stands, my parents are my legal guardians. I can't enter into binding contracts without their permission. As love has me considering the contract of marriage, I vote for change.

When my parents are gone, folks expect that my brothers will take the reins. Well, not if I pull this horse to a dead stop with my own unsupported hands. To be fair, I love my brothers and they have dutifully let me ride on the back of their bikes, four-wheelers, jet skis, mini-bikes and horses, but I am grown now, and not always going their way.

My parents know I am preparing the fields, and working hard to start tipping the scales of justice to include myself. I want to marry. I want to have sex. I have no intention of asking permission. I do not want my brothers to be my keepers. The thought infuriates me. And that's not just my Dutch oven PTSD talking. Why should I be susceptible to their whims? They don't own me. Or do they? What part of the Old Testament law is our society cherry-picking this week concerning rights?

In James Allen's *As A Man Thinketh*, he writes "Law, not confusion, is the dominating principle of the universe; justice, not injustice, is the soul and substance of life; and righteousness, not corruption, is the molding and moving force in the spiritual government of the world. This being so, we have but to right ourselves to find that the universe is right."

Allen further contends, "Circumstances do not make a person, but reveal him." (We must forgive the sexist language of this 1902 author, but such forgiveness is needed, anyway, for righting ourselves to pick the fruit of justice.)

I embrace my purpose. My autistic circumstances reveal me as no neurotypical, privileged, white-girl life would. I am just Barb, and I am grateful. When I write, it flows from the breeze because it is who I am and what I am here to do. Feelings and ideas funnel through the top of my head and grind down in words. The word drip is slow, but as rich as I can brew. Best served hot.

(End excerpt.)

When enough of us embrace our purpose – and being part of the solution – eventually justice prevails and discrimination bails.
And if memory serves as mine does, we are wise not to be too sclerotic and quick to believe everything we think.

Thanks for listening.
Like you, trying to know B

I use stinger suits to navigate deadly Australian jellyfish, Google to get close to spelling ("Do you mean _____?"), and detail oriented editors to write books. Deaf Beethoven made music. Mute Barb stars in podcasts. To those with dyslexia labels: May you find your way through and go where you wish.

Chapter 18

Dyslexia Please

by Lowis Prisslowskee

"The difference between those who fail and those who succeed is largely perseverance. Never quit." Charles Schwab (Mr. Schwab has dyslexia and a foundation providing support for people with learning disabilities... which I think is separate from the money he has for my personal retirement.)

On a recent TV interview, I said NMIH instead of NIMH for National Institute of Mental Health – twice.

No one in my office trusts a phone number I jot down, "Oh, did Lois give you that?"

I couldn't spell restrurant (a place where you pay to eat) or beaurocrat (government official whom you pay to seat), if you had a knife to my mother's throat. (Please don't – she is feisty, and it's sure to get messy.)

Dyslexia runs in families, and many individuals with dyslexia profiles don't hear sounds within words clearly. For example, my Mom's name is Rachel, but she answers to Dad always calling her "Racial," much to the delight of my childhood best buddies, Brian and Steve, who teased me relentlessly about "racial" issues in our lily-white home. At age eighty-four, Dad still can't pronounce "aluminum." It always comes out with a clear "Ah" at the beginning... but then it sounds like a slow-motion train wreck of melting "L"s and "M"s. Dad is good-natured and always attempts his pronunciation nemesis for the well-meaning curious. You should ask him when you see him. It's cute, because the man is no pity party. He is gregarious, charming, physically and mentally strong and agile, funny, an impressive sharpshooter, and he can fix anything – welding, carpentry, mechanical, electrical, plumbing – anything.

When Eli was eight years old, I lost a game of Cranium because I could not spell the word "psychologist" backwards. (I had not been drinking.)

More recently, teenage Eli came across Bhagwan Shree Rajneesh (a would-be biochemical terrorist with a cult following, whose group put salmonella in a small town's salad bars so the townspeople would not be well enough to vote in the elections, thus swinging the vote his way.) This struck our boy as funny, so for a couple of days Eli would refer to himself as "Bhagwan Shree Rajneesh" in third person as he went about his day. As in, "Bhagwan Shree Rajneesh will now get some ice cream." For whatever reason, this cracked us up. Always wanting to participate in a good joke, I tried very hard to recall his new Indian name to summon him to dinner or to take out the trash… to no avail… I simply could not get the name out quickly. I even tried to write it down phonetically to recall it… but, it came out so choppy it was not funny.

I read slowly. I get self-conscious when people can see how often I turn the page. I only take books on planes if I am out of Ambien. And I am never out of Ambien. (Tip #1989 or maybe it's #1898… marry an anesthesiologist… it's now legal in all states.)

I never read fancy menus, because it's too hard and I'm trying to have fun. (Fortunately, I'm not a picky eater, and my wife and best friends are foodies so they love ordering two entrees and we "share.")

I don't do public handwriting. (Graffiti gang tagging, sure, but not handwriting.) It is not safe even in my own home. My wife took a picture of a note I put on the dry erase board on our fridge. In my best handwriting it read,, "Beagle Elopement diet complete = 33lbs! and he looks Great. Dr. Ty Heath promises to uphold her hypocratic oath and Do No Harm by feeding him snacks/people food. Thank you, The Management" (Back story: Ty feeds those she loves, and her table scraps have made over-loved Matthew Beagle sausage shaped. Our chubby beagle waddled off chasing a scent, and got stuck in a drain tube for ten days until he was thin enough to crawl out – Winnie-the-Pooh style). Ty put my poorly spelled refrigerator note on Facebook, which was awkward, as I am trying to earn my living as an educator.

Once a year, for the holidays, I handwrite thank-you notes to about thirty practitioners I get to work with at Psychoeducational Network. It literally takes me five or six hours because each note is different, and in order not to appear like the least-educated person they know and spark a coup, I type out each sentiment, and then copy and re-copy it in cursive – or something pretty close. Our practitioners would probably be happy with the gift card alone, but handwritten thank-you notes are one of those Southern etiquette traditions that stuck with me, like saying "Sir" and "Ma'am" and actually meaning it respectfully. BTW, in trying to find the word "coup" above... I knew what it sounded like – pretty much – and knew it meant "sudden takeover of power or leadership," but my spelling attempts (koo, kue, cue,) were not close enough to gain assistance from Google or spell check. So, I spoke an in-context sentence to my handy-dandy, free, speech-to-text app, "Dragon Dictation," and this came up: "There was a coup to overthrow the government"... and so the chapter continues.

Before I lose all credibility and become a social piranha (another one of my common malapropisms)... let me explain. It's dyslexia, and it's how my brain works, and I am not alone.

The International Dyslexia Association explains, "Dyslexia is a neurologically based, often familial, disorder which interferes with the acquisition and processing of language. Varying in degrees of severity, it is manifested by difficulties in receptive and expressive language, including phonological processing, in reading, writing, spelling, handwriting, and sometimes in arithmetic."

Dyslexia can be hard, especially during the early school years. But once you own your differences, learn strategies, and PERSEVERE, the benefits of this type of mind can be outstanding.

Dyslexia is common. In researching the prevalence, I found that the statistics varied wildly. So, I did some nerd networking and asked "How prevalent?" to my buddy Dr. Rachael Gabriel, author of *Reading's Non-Negotiables,* who has an incredibly specific Ph.D. (and I quote), "I do reading – period."

Rachael responded to my text question in this email in less than five minutes. She is clearly excited about what she does… and she sports a non-dyslexic brain.

"…Hi!

For political correctness, I'd use the International Dyslexia Association stats in general, but they sidestep this just by saying 15-20% of the population has learning disabilities... 70-80% of those are reading disabilities, and most of that group is dyslexic, and they leave you to do the math (which is super lame and unhelpful) and works out to "most of" 10-16% of the population... So, in articles written by responsible folks, I often see 5-10% BUT IT DEPENDS... and the responsible folks explain why it depends.

So, for safety and clarity, I always present the full range of estimates and say why those estimates are so fuzzy and unreliable. Something like: Estimates of prevalence depend on the particular definition of dyslexia used in the study, and commonly range from 5% to 10% of the population. Because of discrepancies in definitions, and identification criteria, an estimate of prevalence is specific to a particular sample and to the definition used in a study. For example, some professionals view dyslexia as a continuum of ability/disability, and others as a discrete diagnostic category, and many use varying cutoff points for determining a diagnosis…"

Let's just say, Rachael kept writing. It is good to have detail-oriented people in your life for those "responsible," "politically correct," and "safe" moments.

For this moment, let's just go with 10% and move on. (Individuals with dyslexia are often good at seeing the big picture and not getting bogged down in details.)

Experts estimate that about 10% of the population are dyslexic.

Sally Shaywitz, M.D., co-director of the Yale Center for Dyslexia and Creativity, with her husband Bennett Shaywitz, M.D., clarifies that "dyslexia is not an all-or-nothing phenomenon, but like hypertension and obesity, occurs in varying degrees of severity." The Shaywitzes also authored the "Sea of Strengths" model, which emphasizes the statistically significant prevalence of critical thinking and creativity skills in individuals with dyslexia. Furthermore, their pioneering research confirms both the universality of this type of mind in every language, and functional magnetic resonance imaging (fMRI) data reveal the neurological signature of dyslexia, thus making it no longer be a "hidden disability."

In dyslexia, one may be a slow reader but a fast thinker. For example, in writing this book, I researched maybe a hundred books. How did I do that? Audiobooks – usually on double speed if a conversational narrative; 1.5 speed if the content is more dense. I reserve regular speed for authors I particularly respect, and who read aloud their own book – I find the teaching rather intimate.

(It's fun to hear Bill Clinton, Rachel Maddow, or Temple Grandin tell me what they think right into my ears. Okay, maybe Dr. Rachel Maddow most of all – but I digress. For more on that logic, please see the gay chapter. How people speak is also fascinating to me. That is one of the things I love about being a psychologist – hearing people's stories in their own words. I am curious to know more about them and their experiences. While curiosity is not exclusive to individuals with dyslexia, it is one of the many strengths associated with this type of processing. As Dorothy Parker writes, "The cure for boredom is curiosity. There is no cure for curiosity." And that is great news.)

Another good thing about ear learning is that like many individuals with ADHD and dyslexia, I think best when moving. I listen to books when I jog, wash dishes, fold laundry, drive, walk dogs, or change light bulbs (kidding, I am Polish so I never change light bulbs... alone, that is... plus as a psychologist I know they must want to change). I pause the audiobook when I get an "aha" moment, and Dragon Dictate myself an email of the idea, which I then insert into my writing later. Then I move on... preserving my short-term-memory real estate. I should also note that when I find an audiobook particularly illuminating, I order the print version too, so I can skim the text later to refresh my memory and practice those fresh ideas for solutions with my clients. (So, you are welcome, smart writers – because I actually buy two copies of your books.)

Many more academic strategies helpful for the dyslexic processing style are outlined in *Overcoming Dyslexia: A New and Complete*

Science-Based Program for Reading Problems at Any Level by Sally Shaywitz, M.D. It is available in audiobook. It is a methodical program based in empirical research, prescribing lots of direct, structured practice and considerable frequent assessment of fluency and comprehension. Pre-reading and re-reading, and relevant cartoon drawing – summarizing concepts or possible essay question answers – are also presented, along with writing, penmanship, and keyboarding recommendations. Shaywitz also encourages children to record themselves reading aloud.

The main point of this chapter is to drop the shame and use what we know to improve lives. Below is an observation-and-recommendations report I wrote for Ava, a bright, eight-year-old third grader who is struggling with the hard parts of dyslexia. I include this because I hope readers will understand that identification of and support for dyslexia need not be haphazard nor deficit based. Best practices can be uplifting and even fun.

We practitioners who serve individuals with dyslexia are wise to remember that our recommendations may change a child's life. It is critical that we present findings in an empowering way.

Ava's case and report below are real, and may provide a template for others, as this multi-step approach worked out exceptionally well for the child, family, school, and support professionals. Positive feedback from all parties is included below.

If we can help children like Ava understand that these difficulties can be overcome, and that dyslexics are often unusually high-level conceptualizers – and are thus over-represented in highly successful positions requiring non-linear thinking – we may empower untold perseverance and innovation. **Hang in there – the long-term outcome is GREAT – because you can learn to read, but it is very difficult to learn creativity and outside-the-box thinking.** As Rumi recommends, "Live life as if everything is rigged in your favor."

Here is the report:
Observations and educational considerations for Ava [Her name was changed for privacy – and dyslexic ease. Plus, I added a few sassy comments in brackets to connect back to you readers]:

Dyslexics have trouble differentiating "phonemes," which are the smallest units of language. This difficulty is a major contributor to slowing down the speed and accuracy of reading, writing, spelling, handwriting, speaking, and memory.

Functional magnetic resonance imaging (fMRI) reveals clear differences in the ways that dyslexic and non-dyslexic individuals process written words. Fluid readers process written language in the left hemisphere, and literally show proportionately larger left hemispheres; whereas individuals with dyslexia use predominantly the right hemisphere, but use multiple areas of the brain to process written language – so they physically have more symmetrical hemispheres.

These differences lead to many dyslexic advantages and considerable strengths, such as: holistic perception; outside-the-box thinking; three-dimensional spatial reasoning; mechanical aptitude; the ability to perceive relationships like analogies, metaphors, paradoxes, similarities, differences, implications, gaps, and imbalances; and processing subtle patterns in complex and constantly shifting systems. [Individuals with dyslexia are often very good at understanding interconnections and relationships, and thus making predictions. Perhaps this makes for decent psychologists – even if they can't spell the word backwards.]

While all individuals with dyslexia vary, these skills are statistically reliable in this population and are huge assets in many careers. In fact, entrepreneurs are five times as likely to be dyslexic as not. Being able to see the big picture and not get lost in details helps dyslexics flourish in the world of business.

School psychologist Dr. Stephanie Carroll's psychoeducational assessment finds that Ava shows signs of classic dyslexia. Ava clearly demonstrates many of the aforementioned strengths and challenges that go with dyslexic processing.

I HIGHLY recommend that your family read the following books – both are available in audiobook. [How do you think I know all this?]

Neurodiversity: Discovering the Extraordinary Gifts of Autism, ADHD, Dyslexia, and Other Brain Differences by Thomas Armstrong

The Dyslexic Advantage: Unlocking the Hidden Potential of the Dyslexic Brain by Brock and Fernette Eide

It is wise to build on Ava's considerable strengths when considering the best educational placement for her. Both days of observations supported Dr. Carroll's findings. Ava is bright, physically active, and athletic, but she struggles significantly with classic dyslexic symptoms. Ava is very aware of her weaknesses and was observed to hide those struggles in a variety of ways. [Please see the addendum at the close of this book for the actual observation summaries, to help demonstrate how multi-day, multi-setting data can benefit client care.]

Takeaway on Dyslexia and a note on Autism:
Due to a different pattern of brain organization, the dyslexic brain is wired inefficiently for reading, writing, and spelling. But on the flip side of this neurological coin are quantifiable advantages. Brock and Fernette Eide's book, *The Dyslexic Advantage: Unlocking the Hidden Potential of the Dyslexic Brain,* breaks these empirical facts down into four distinct talents that are statistically significant for individuals with dyslexia, using the acronym M.I.N.D.:

M: Material thinking – mentally visualizing three-dimensional relationships. These thinkers are overrepresented in dyslexia-rich professions, including engineers, artists, designers, mathematicians, and builders. In fact, dyslexia is so common at Massachusetts Institute of Technology (MIT) that the founder of the MIT media lab, Nicholas Negroponte (a dyslexic himself) called it the MIT disease in his autobiography.

I: Interconnected thinking – seeing connections, rather than facts in isolation, making for terrific entrepreneurs (35% of entrepreneurs in the USA have dyslexia), comedians, psychologists, and lawyers, as everything is about relationships and discerning relevant information.

N: Narrative thinking – storytelling abilities to construct mental scenes from fragmented memories, contributing to outstanding authors, speakers, and directors.

D: Dynamic Thinking – ability to make predictions (past and future), based on incomplete information or episodic simulation. Such creative, "best fit" predictions are priceless in fields such as anthropology, science, and investment planning (Thanks again, Charles Schwab.)

The Eides go on to highlight Dr. Manuel Casanova's groundbreaking cell-to-cell, neuronal-connections brain research at the University of Kentucky School of Medicine. Casanova identified key features that show the structural ways that neurons in the brain vary with "conditions." For example, the microcircuitry differences between individuals with autism and dyslexia labels are profound: "Individuals with tightly spaced minicolumns (cells in the cortex that are organized into columns of functional units) tended to form more connections between nearby minicolumns, while individuals with broadly spaced minicolumns tended to form more connections between minicolumns in distant parts of the brain." Meaning: "The brains of individuals with autism are biased toward short connections at the expense of long connections – just the opposite with dyslexia." So, my dear Barb excels at fine-detail processing, which is performed in one highly localized area at a time. "In contrast, joining distant areas of the brain together is what individuals with dyslexia do best. As a result, individuals with dyslexia excel at drawing ideas from anything and anywhere, and at connecting different concepts together."

These two brain types complement each other. Neither may be a result of purposeless breakdown in function, but rather a valuable specialization trade-off.

So if you are dyslexic, it is wise to find autistic friends and business partners.

Some Resources to Consider:

*Listen = Learning Ally is a national non-profit that provides people with access to thousands of audio titles through a monthly membership. Originally conceived of as Recording for the Blind, Learning Ally serves a much broader audience today – hello ear-readers! I recommend we drop the eye-reader snobbery. Print is not always the best way for everybody to learn. There are three types of reading: eye, ear, and fingers (Braille). As Ben Foss writes, "Focusing on eye reading overlooks the real goals of education, which are learning, independent thinking, and mastering the ability to make new connections in the world of ideas." **Let's not be print snobs. There are other intellectually valid ways for information absorption and comprehension.**

*Susan = Susan Barton is an internationally recognized dyslexia expert, and she is literally in the International Dyslexia Hall of Fame. On a Coffee Klatch podcast (this Special Needs Radio organization is a great resource for information about dyslexia and dysgraphia), I heard Barton make the generous offer to email her at susan@brightsolutions.com, and she will give you advice on how to present information about a child's dyslexia based on the child's age. Her website, www.brightsolutions.com, is also packed with free tips that are easily accessible to all visitors. The site has a visible "to listen" option, which allows the visitor to highlight the text and hear the content. Much information is also presented in video format.

*Accommodate. Accommodations are important. Sally Shaywitz's internationally best-selling book, *Overcoming Dyslexia: A New and Complete Science-Based Program for Reading Problems at Any Level*, presents an exhaustive list of accommodations, and the logic behind each, that may be a catalyst for your success.

*Technology. I recommend making technology your new best friend (along with a non-verbal autistic mute or two.)

*Empower. Educate yourself about getting better at being dyslexic. Some empowering videos on dyslexia education are:
　　Ben Foss's "Choose Strengths, Not Shame": June 23, 2014, Tedx Sonoma = http://bit.ly/1MJIvg0
　　And
　　Tiffany Sunday's "The Gift of Innovation and Entrepreneurial Mind": Tedx Turtle Creek Women = http://bit.ly/1NxCRiJ

*You = You are the most significant resource in being successful with your neurodiversity. Focus on your gifts – what we focus on grows.

Spend more time developing areas where you excel. We know that many individuals with dyslexia are outstanding in areas such as: curiosity, creativity, athletics, design, people skills, delegation, comedy, logical skills, and mechanical abilities. Prize what you can do and master that, while outsourcing what you can't do efficiently. How can you put your gifts to work?

Just B.

Chapter 19

Two Bs
by Barb Rentenbach

"If you can't fly then run, if you can't run then walk, if you can't walk then crawl, but whatever you do you have to keep moving forward." Dr. Martin Luther King, Jr.

Life is a balance of two B's:

1. Just being and
2. Being just.

In *I Might Be You: An Exploration of Autism and Connection*, I wrote much of the bounty of just being. Here is an excerpt, sharing how just being can connect you with another without language: "We are not hiding. You search with limited senses, and therefore our humanity is camouflaged to you. Be still. Be quiet. Be. We notice you on the glacier. We observe you completely. Language presentation is the barrier to our friendship – not sentience or intellect. We do not speak your language, but you can speak ours. Be still. Be quiet. Be. And now be with us. Our silent and invisible language is that easy to learn. Feel it? Welcome. Our friendship has begun."

I have always been good at just being. I know now that to fully be, one must also do. This truth comes with the added bonus that doing can be a real calorie burner. But wait, there is more.

Those who are good at just being are fully present, and see justly that change is often needed to be just. (That may read more clearly when held up to a mirror.)

Change is always a chain reaction. Google tells us that a chain reaction is "a chemical reaction or other process in which the products themselves promote or spread the reaction, which under certain conditions may accelerate dramatically."

If you seek change, make your move. Humanity needs exactly you.

Consider, for example, Buddhist monk Quang Duc's self-immolation on a Saigon street in June 1963, which led to the November 1963 overthrow of the Diem regime in South Vietnam, a government that infamously persecuted Buddhists, thus ending the "Buddhist crisis." Fellow monk and prolific author Thich Nhat Hanh, in a conversation with Dr. Martin Luther King, explained that this was not an act of suicide. Quang Duc immolated himself out of love, and wanting equality of justice – not out of despair or self-pity. It was hard to be heard in Vietnam at that time, but Quang Duc was heard around the changing world.

The change chain grew stronger as photographers, pigeons, and presidents bound and reacted.

Patrick Witty's *Time Magazine* article, on the fiftieth anniversary of Quang Duc's burn, interviewed Malcolm Browne, who photographed the event and won a Pulitzer prize for his international reporting, as well as the World Press Photo of the Year award.

Browne recalled, "The main thing on my mind was getting the pictures out. I realized this is something of unusual importance and that I'd have to get them to the AP in one of its far-flung octopus tentacles as soon as possible. And I also knew this was a very difficult thing to do in Saigon on short notice. The whole trick was to get it to some transmission point. We had to get the raw film shipped by airfreight, or some way. It was not subject to censorship at that point. We used a pigeon to get it as far as Manila. And in Manila they had the apparatus to send it by radio."

Patrick Witty then asked: "When you say pigeon, what do you mean exactly?"

Browne said, "A pigeon is a passenger on a regular commercial flight whom you have persuaded to carry a little package."

This famous picture appeared on President Kennedy's desk that day. As a result of many just doing their part, Thich Quang Duc's self-immolation changed the world.

We do not all need to burn up; but we must share our fire if we want change.

Warren Buffett says, "Someone's sitting in the shade today because someone planted a tree a long time ago." I used to just sit in the shade; now I am trying to sow just seeds so you may too.

Growing change is often hard. The United States recently swore in a black attorney general named Lynch. And I am a gainfully employed "severely autistic" mute. It was not easy for Loretta Lynch or Barb Rentenbach, but here we are, being heard.

Since my last book, I assiduously clicked out my ability to type independently, and took the opportunity to make changes in my twenty-four/seven care and immerse myself in my chosen career. I am a freelance neurodiversity promoter. It is a growing field, providing relevant shade for perhaps the largest minority in the world. Steve Silberman wrote in *Neuro Tribes: The Legacy of Autism and the Future of Neurodiversity*, "There are roughly as many people on the spectrum in America as there are Jews." For posterity, I note that Silberman's book came out as I was finishing this book. The importance of *Neuro Tribes* resonated in our neurodiversity community immediately, so I put my editors on hold, read his book, and then completed this chapter.

As with Malcolm Browne, for many of us, the main thing on our mind is getting the pictures out, because we realize that "this is something of unusual importance." Each day, I step out of my autistic darkroom to capture images. Before I am overexposed, I return to my safelight autistic sanctuary to process. I wordlessly calculate what to develop and dilute. What appears in my developer tray is my neurochemical art. I then treat myself to a stop bath before the arduous task of getting my product to the neurotypical market. Next, I persuade my index-finger pigeon to peck out my little package.

In wide-awake Mark Nepo's book, *Hold Nothing Back: Essentials for an Authentic Life,* he teaches the interplay between effort and grace. Since one never knows when effort will turn to grace, he creates this way: "I push the pen until it pulls me."

To fly majestically as designed, we must pump our wings until we catch the current. Thus, to be our highest selves, we must balance our wings with being and doing. For me, doing is VERY hard. This chapter alone took over six months. To show for it, I have a swollen arm with broken, bloody, seeping skin from where I bite my right wrist violently, and then bang it into my teeth as forcefully as I can with my dominant left hand, while caterwauling like an petrified alley cat. I warn others to get back as best I can, but they don't always get my non-verbal message – and in this state I am sure to grab, claw and bite you if you get too close.

Do I want to be like this? Is this Autism? I am not sure. From what I have gathered, "severely autistic" may describe my way of being and doing as accurately as words can at this time.

I don't know how to write about injustice and anguish without feeling it. So, I bite into pain, knowing that Grace will come. The consistent, eventual reward and bliss of Grace fuels my perseverance and keeps me moving.

I planned to end this chapter and book with a rah-rah for you to keep being and doing, as Grace will come.

Then my perception changed. Two days ago, I was just being on my smooth wooden swing, on a faultless fall afternoon, sensorily relishing remnants of my favorite microwave buttered popcorn on my fingers and cheeks, when I captured the image of Grace. Astonishing! But how? My autistic darkroom was closed. Grace was not out there. Grace was in here. Like Malcolm Brown, "I realized this is something of unusual importance and that I'd have to get them to the AP in one of its far-flung octopus tentacles as soon as possible. And I also knew this was a very difficult thing to do" in AUTISM, on short notice.

For immediate release: See past octopus ink – Grace is always everywhere.

Practical Implications:

1. Initiating action to be just comes less naturally to me than just being. So I use "excellerants." I have learned to purposely connect with doer types whose excess energy sparks my light. My dear Smother, or Elke, or SS, may burn too intensely for your tastes – mine too, often – but it takes sustained heat to ignite my doing. Experiment with connections, and discover who complements you. The chemical composition is right

when they grow branches from your tree, too, blooming each of you and producing more shade.

2. When asked my opinion on the Autism Speaks controversy, I usually give a quick/kind response like "not political but very active B" because typing takes me so long, and sustained negative emotions make me physically ill. My plan has always been to help unify in other ways. In 2012, I wrote my intentions to my publicist: "I plan on writing many books in myriad genres, each creatively unique in process and form. 'Autism Advocate' will not be my only title; eventually my musings will inspire mainstreamers, and that will serve my ASD clan best. My work and person will change ASD inside and outside."

   My sense is that it is true that we are no longer willing to be spectators in our own stories. Our process is our story. You see, we are all teachers of our own story. For best results: Teach from the heart to the heart. To unify our love, we all must actively seek to know other stories. Thank you all for teaching your stories and doing your fair share to make the appreciation of neurodiversity more common than juice stains in minivans.

3. A final thought on change. Zoom Autism magazine asked me, "How do you deal with change?" Previously, notable change (like a key staff member leaving) would put me into a dizzying tailspin of anxiety, uncertainty, and frustration (meaning: I would regress, bite, scream, grab, and smear and eat feces. Focusing on work would not be possible until a set schedule and structure were again established – sometimes taking months.) These days, I have learned to respond differently. I do not react immediately; I study. (Okay, to be honest, this time, I still did plenty of biting, smearing, and aggressive grabs... but this time... I kept moving forward and made sure to include others in my struggle.)

SS turned me on to this concept of "never worrying alone." She stole the idea from Edward Hallowell's book, *Driven to Distraction at*

Work: How to Focus and Be More Productive. Hallowell recommends:

"You just have to find someone you like and trust. My basic three-step method of worry control is as follows:

1. Never worry alone.
2. Get the facts. (Toxic worry is rooted in wrong information, lack of information, or both.)
3. Make a plan. Having a plan reduces feelings of vulnerability and increases feelings of control."

For me this strategy became possible a few years ago, when I was finally able to make and sustain real "non-paid friends." I wrote about how friends came to be in *I Might Be You: An Exploration of Autism and Connection.*

Recently when my house manager of four years gave her two-week notice, instead of going inward and letting my fecund, catastrophizing imagination ruin my mental and physical health, I chose to connect and problem-solve with two old friends and my parents. That decision to reach out immediately had me feeling empowered and supported.

That is why the "Ask Barb" portion of my work is so important. (In the following Appendix, please find several actual "Ask Barb" questions and responses, featured on my LOUD MUTE RADIO show.) I want to make it safe and easy for others to reach out, so that they are not alone in worrying and finding solutions. Life is a balance of aloneness and togetherness. We all need both.

Trusted friend Just B

I can see more from here.

Chapter 20 Conclusion:
Neurodiversity is More Than
Good – It's God, and is By Design
by Barb Rentenbach

"On this path, effort never goes to waste, and there is no failure. Even a little effort toward spiritual awareness will protect you from the greatest fear." The Bhagavad Gita 2:40

I have a lot of fears. I have a lot of stuff: Autism, Echolalia, Cellulite, Psoriasis, Good Hair (What? Folk should know), Ataxia, Apraxia, One-eyed-cave-fish quality vision, and Purpose. That last one is key, and I think is the Golden Mean. When you remember your purpose, you are able to use your stuff to know and do – as in the old joke, "Knowledge is knowing a tomato is a fruit; wisdom is not putting it in a fruit salad."

Patterns were my first love. (I was born addicted to carbs, so I am not counting that.) A fractal is a mathematical set that typically displays self-similar patterns. Like me – like you, a fractal is a never-ending pattern.

The cosmos follows the Golden Ratio of patterns and was recalled by Leonardo Fibonacci around 1200 and works like this: 0, 1, 1, 2, 3, 5, 8, 13, 21, 34, 55 and so on forever. Each number is the sum of the two numbers that precede it. It's a simple pattern, but it appears to be a kind of built-in numbering system to the universe. At first glance, I do not resemble you the elegant proportions in Da Vinci's Vitruvian Man, but with the Golden Rule, everyone's perfect pattern is revealed.

This book is fractal art.

I leave autism on a work visa to know more of the grand design. I learned, while struggling to peck out my last book, that I am no longer content to spend my life conically in my autism, as symmetrically beautiful as it may be. I climb this inverted mountain not because it is there, but because you are there – and I reach out to know you, and you me.

My Smiling Shrink, SS (aka Lois), often digs in to tug me on when I slide back unscheduled to microscopia by bringing me news from the macro world of psychology that she thinks I will find tempting. For example, she bounced in with a book on the benefits of Dyslexia. She is always looking for the positive side of things. But, I'm still waiting for the rosy side of my psoriasis to be revealed. *The Dyslexia Advantage: Unlocking the Hidden Potential of the Dyslexic Brain* is by Brock Eide, M.D., and Fernette Eide, M.D. They are married. Apparently same-specialty marriages are legal up north. The Eides do not dispute that the dyslexic brain is wired inefficiently for reading, writing, and spelling. They simply move past that and use empirical data to support that dyslexia is not just a type of learning disability, but a systemic style of processing that has quantifiable advantages. The Eides outline **M.I.N.D.** strengths for individuals with Dyslexia: advanced abilities in **M**aterial Reasoning, **I**nterconnected Reasoning, **N**arrative or Story-Based Reasoning, and **D**ynamic Reasoning. It is an uplifting and motivating perspective.

I have written extensively on the two sides of the autistic neurological coin, and SS loves positive psychology, so we began brainstorming about writing this book about neurodiversity. Specifically, our plan was to cover dyslexia, autism, homosexuality, anxiety, and ADHD. SS has more of these differences than I, so I played the "normal" this time around.

Two hours after we made this happy plan, somebody with perspectives not shared by most, set off two bombs at the Boston Marathon, wreaking untallied horror and destruction. Our premise that diversity of brains, like biodiversity, is by design then needed to expand to explore the dual-edged sword of this nature.

The individuals who set those explosions thought they were doing the right thing – right by them, right by justice, right by war, right by revenge, right by might… something. Perspectives are often hard to understand. But we must try, as illumination is the key to prevention and healing.

So what happened for those who chose to harm at such a level? Are they Godless? I am not certain it is possible to be "Godless." Can any fleck of God be without its Primary component? I think not.

I believe those who commit acts of terror... got disconnected. As a non-verbal autistic, I can relate to that. Loneliness is the most predominant side effect of our unique design. Many times, autistics revert to isolation by default rather than preference. It is infinitely easier to back away and not try to be included instead of oafishly stepping in and attempting to convey you intend to be a part.

Once one feels separated, it is easy for hopelessness and anger to flood in and dilute knowing we are all the same.

Hope is knowing Now is built on Yesterday's learning. As Sandy Hook Elementary was finally enough repetition of wasteful tragedy for us to collectively take action about gun control, perhaps we can learn to treat terrorism in a prophylactically fresh way also. Together, we may help prevent the isolation and disconnection that lead to acts of terror. I believe God cares about all of us through all of us. Reach out and connect with those who may be struggling with separation. It takes just one person to care to change a life for the positive. Be that for someone.

Donna Williams, one of the most prolific and respected artists concerning autism and neurodiversity, writes "In my world it's a place of patterns and feelings. In my world it's a haven for what is real. It's my world, nobody can steal it, but people like me, we live in the shadows."

I'm planning well-lit fractal "Aut Art" galleries.

Although my mind has never been very popular, I intend to have the popular mind know our autistic perception – a world of detail that reveals the grand design. Autism is our prism, not our prison.

The danger in absorbing this book is that you may see everything differently. (Most see me as smarter and thinner already.) You risk the loss of your comfortable position, as noticing the tartan pattern of the universe illuminates our undeniable clan connection.

My thoughts on differences are clear. It is in our best interest to remember that we are all the same. People are flecks of God. Each God fragment, dispersed through space/time, has a slightly different shape. One shape is not superior to another. All are necessary to complete the perfect, infinite God puzzle. To be proud that one "tolerates" diversity is ludicrous. The whole system is the sum of its parts. Be your part. Connect with other parts and the God puzzle is revealed.

Knowing with you, B

Appendix I
Ask Barb Transcript

This is an example of an "ASK BARB" question-and-answer from the transcript of our Loud Mute Radio podcast.

For More "ASK BARB" questions and answers about such topics as special-needs financial planning, sexuality, aggression, anxiety, pyschoeducational assessments, communication, friendships, finding purpose, and more, please tune in to Loud Mute Radio.

"Ask Barb" Segment from Show 18 "Lessons from Teens on Gaming with Jennifer Ho-Dougatz"

Lois = And we are back with "ASK BARB." Evan, please read Hannah's email.

Evan = Okay, first here is what Hannah posted on Facebook:
"If you've not experienced the joy and enlightenment of hearing the perpetually silenced yet stubbornly shouted voice of a non-normative communicator, please, PLEASE get to know the powerful advocate and educator Barb Rentenbach through her podcast/radio show called Loud Mute Radio!!!"

Lois = So Barb then friended Hannah, and Barb and she had the following exchange.

Evan = Hannah wrote: "I just listened to your first episode and immediately forwarded it to my son's entire school team. I feel like I am in the fight of my life, trying to get them to see ALL of who and what he is. Your words and the words of Jess Wilson have been a rallying force and powerful directive for me of late. I cannot express how truly grateful I am for your words and your passion!!! All my love and blessings to you."

Lois = Thank you, Evan. That helps set the stage for Hannah's serious question. Eli, please read the next email from Hannah.

Eli = Subject: ID vs ASD Conundrum

Hi, Barb (and Lois!) –

For the sake of brevity I will forsake my adulations and praise, excepting this one comment: YOU ROCK!!!

Serious question... How do you (and all your widely varied friends and colleagues) feel about an ID (Intellectually Disabled) diagnosis combined with and/or compared with an ASD diagnosis? All our private clinicians and therapists say my son is Autistic. The School Psych says he is Autistic AND Intellectually Disabled as well. (He is nine years old, verbal with a speech delay and a LOT of Echolalia, and he has never in over six years on an IEP had an ID label applied to him or even hinted at by any of his teachers or specialists.) We believe this diagnosis is really inaccurate and could be very detrimental to his educational progress. I want something to strengthen our case without just relying on a competing evaluator's assessment. Because, let's face it, standardized tests mean exactly dick for most people.

So, I guess what I'm basically asking is – How do we argue for a person's intelligence, abilities, and potential when confronted with myopic or bigoted individuals and bureaucracies like this? I'm fighting for his dignity, humanity, and an expectation of competence and I feel I'm losing ground :-((

Please help us turn the tide!

Anyway, I was just searching for some insight and support from people who have been down this road before us. Thanks a bunch as always!!! I am in love with Loud Mute

Radio!!!

T's Momma

Barb = let me ask my mother first. Smother, Please share your own thoughts and advice regarding Hannah's question.

Smother = Hello, T's Momma!!

Gosh!! I wish I had the magic words for you on this question!! Barb also had a diagnosis of MR (mentally retarded). Guess ID (intellectual disability) is the new, "nicer" phrase now. We never believed or accepted that for a minute: she was too clever, too crafty, too curious. I believe that curiosity is a sign of intellect – she was always taking things apart or trying to figure out how to get away, and other traits that we knew were intelligence in her – we just didn't know how to get it out!

To answer your question, though, is very difficult. I would suggest that you go to any of your meetings armed with studies and references from colleges, medical schools, autism associations, and autistic people who have been known to exhibit intelligence after a particular key was found to unlock it. Like the real Rainman, Temple Grandin, Donna Williams, or Barb! Remember in the '70s, '80s, and even '90s when Barb was coming along, there were either no or few studies being done. We had to fight the school system for so many years; it was long and frustrating, but eventually certain teachers/psychologists and administrators came our way. You have the benefit of having so much more awareness and studies being done.

It's hard to have to wait, but there will be other years where different people come into your life for T. I know there is turnover in schools, and in your searching for other specialists, there will be special ones that enter. I might advocate for a different psychologist or a supervisor... anything to get away from the one that is blocking you. I fully support you in this quest because we have been there.

I have said this before, but in a frustrating situation, try to take the long view... next year or two, T may have new teachers, a new school? New specialists? A new key to his showing what he can do? Take heart in that things don't stand still. You sound like a great advocate for your child. Keep fighting and challenging the system, and don't be too disheartened about the now. I wish I could have given more specific advice; it's just that systems are hard to deal with, and we have to be armed for the long haul. I wish you the best of efforts to deal with this – and my unwavering support!!

Barb = SS?

Lois = You want my advice? Wow. Okay, thanks.

Chad, please insert Leonard Nimoy clip here = Spock: "I need your advice." Bones: "You want advice from me? I need a drink. "Spock: I do not joke, doctor."

Lois = Hannah, "ID" (Intellectually Disabled) is the New DSM-5 revised term which replaces "MR" (mentally retarded). The idea was to encourage more comprehensive assessment. The MR diagnosis was based solely on standardized testing – IQ tests, which were designed by walky-talky psychologists like myself and weighted heavily on language. Remember, Barb writes a lot about having the MR diagnosis along with her Autism diagnosis. One of the first things we did was to try and demonstrate her considerable ability… but the IQ tests were so language based. So we basically deconstructed the Stanford-Binet IQ test as best as we could and had Barb make her multiple choice by picking up an easily held object beside each card written in HUGE letters. (Mrs. Rentenbach, do you remember that? I remember, on your kitchen balcony, having Barb demonstrate that to you on math problems, if memory serves.) Anyway, back to your son's ID diagnosis. ID is assessed by both clinical and standardized testing – meaning they measure three domains:

1. Conceptual (like school stuff – language, knowledge, reading, memory, and math),
2. Social (empathy, social judgments, and the ability to make and maintain friendships), and 3. Practical (self care, organizing school or work tasks).

Here is where it gets murky, and we practitioners must learn from people like Barb – judging social areas like empathy and the ability to make friends is hard to do well with individuals who struggle with language. Barb has written extensively on this, and I direct you to a blog she wrote called "Solomon says," where she writes an open letter to one of her favorite authors and thinkers, Andrew Solomon, about how individuals with autism labels are often wrongfully perceived as not being able to understand social cues. Barb debunks that. Likewise, she now has made and maintains several friendships – but it took decades because, as she wrote, "Loneliness is the most predominant side effect of our design" – meaning which comes first, the chicken or the egg – because she did not have friends did not mean she did not want them – it was just hard to communicate and thus hard to attain.

Let me recommend to T's team another possible part of the solution. The UNIT, as it is called, is the "Universal Nonverbal Intelligence Test (UNIT). It is an IQ test designed specifically for individuals with language problems – elective or selective mutes, other cultures, or Autism. Dr. Steve McCallum is the creator, and I am so proud to say that he is part of our practice at Psychoeducational Network. You may wish to view and have T's team check out a brief video by Dr. McCallum on our web site, www.psychoeducational network.com. I hope that helps.

Lois = Thanks, Barb. Okay, Mrs. Rentenbach, will you please read Barb's thoughts on the matter.

Smother = Barb wrote:

Dear Hannah, please share this excerpt from "I Might Be You: An Exploration of Autism and Connection" with T's team. You will find it on page 12 of your new copy. I saw that you bought an ebook this week– I keep track of such things. Thank you. And, if you think it will help, I will send free audiobooks to T's entire team and class. I love being heard. With you, B.

1. **Give us the benefit of the doubt**. Don't assume mental retardation based on behavior and poor communication. One has nothing to lose by assuming competence, and treating the different person with non-patronizing respect. Give us the freedom to rise to expectations – surpassing them may come next.
2. **Get to know us.** That should be the first order of business – not trying to fix or change us. Let the autistic person know that you are here for them and want to get to know who they are and what they do. Everybody has this knowledge about self, although most have

it hidden under a bushel. Autistics traditionally have huge bushels weighting down their heads. It is challenging, but all are capable of discovering who they are and what they do. Let it shine.

3. **Listen.** With nonverbal or echolalic autistics, this seems daunting, but break it down. To listen means to make an effort to hear, take notice of, or heed. So, if folks are not talking or typing – observe. Study their past, their proclivities, and how they spend their time. Find out what gives them joy. Once at least one interest is pinpointed, go from there and make learning opportunities and socialization related to that interest. For me, I was interested in history, science, and philosophy. I actually typed that fact many years ago, but that information was enough to get the ball rolling. Through books on tape and reading aloud, my curiosity came alive. Next, we slowly incorporated my discussing the readings with Lois or a tutor. To discuss, I had to type, so that increased my mental "on-task time," communication skills, and reason to roll out of bed.

Lois = Thank you all. Mrs. Rentenbach, please end the show with Barb's note.

Smother = Note from Barb – "Remember, friends, LMR may not have a show every week in March because most of my pecking this month is focused on finishing a book. But stay tuned, as Dr. Temple Grandin agreed to do the show. Love working hard with u, B."

Chad please insert song 3 pokemon clip from 4:21-4:33 to hear, "I'm on a master plan. I want the whole world to see. I'm gonna be the very best. All I have got to do is believe in me." = https://www.youtube.com/watch?v=hm2eNofu7y8

Chad please end show with Leonard Nimoy clip #9 = "Live long and prosper."

Mule and Muse Productions peeps at my annual lake house birthday party. From left to right: Mike Rentenbach, Jerry Richardson, me (looking fantastic at fourty-three), Carol Holloway, Andrea Lyles, Catie Lauderdale, Kristin Toussaint, Ty Heath, Charlie Morton, Ed Holbrook, Jennifer Ho Dougatz, Aidan Ho, Eli Prislovsky Warwick, Nir Dougatz, Chad Dougatz, and on tube - Smother and SS.

Appendix II
Zooming
by Barb and Lois

The following interview was conducted by Zoom Magazine. The glossy photo shoot version may be found free on line at www.zoomautism.org. With Zoom's munificent blessing we offer it here to boost readers' understanding of ourselves and our intentions. Thank you for your interest. Affectionately, Your Mule and Muse (aka Lois and Barb respectively)

ZOOM: In 10 words or less, how would you describe one another?

B = Straightforward, loyal, perseverant, playful, hardworking, well-loved, funny, and stupidly honest.

L = Complicated, imaginative, dedicated, spiritual, wise, honorable, grateful, witty, and PATIENT.

Zoom: Barb, what was your childhood like?

B = Jam-packed. Now that I schedule my own life, I thrive in a more enjoyable pace. Smother ran my childhood, and it was a marathon sprint. At seventy, she still chooses that pace. My childhood was a whirlwind of every kind of therapy you can imagine and some you can't. Smother had me try everything, as long as it had little probability of lasting harm. My Barbara Ruth body showed up for it all. My Barb mind was more selective. Smother put the Hell in "Helicopter" parent. It was a lot to process. In addition to educational and therapeutic requirements, lil' Barbara Ruth was expected to participate in family gatherings, travel, church and countless sports to the best of her ability. This kid snow skied, ice skated, rode horses, tandem bicycled, and zoomed on dirt bikes. Where there is a will, there is a way. Smother made sure I had a will. Did all that stimulation help? Absolutely! I had to practice doing and being more every single day. Today, dividends from Smother and DD's (Darling Dad) Barbara Ruth investments of love are my greatest wealth. I don't know why I was allotted such a life bounty, but I intend to make the major efforts to give back. I'll probably let tandem biking go; I never pedaled anyway.

Zoom: Barb, are there always words in your head ready to come out?

B = Nope. I think in senses, not sentences. For example, I can hardly imagine having enough strength in this typing finger to explain how I process color – each and every shade and hue has a distinct taste, smell, sound, texture, and feeling. My physical eyes carry a "legally blind" sentence, but light shines through and the party begins. It took me decades to translate sensations into words. Language is not efficient communication for me, but alas it is the only socially acceptable channel at this time. Like my typing, human evolution is slow. Luckily for me I am PATIENT, as advertised.

Thinking and typing in language are the hardest things I do, and I do them every day.

> I use typing to understand my own mind, and that which seems external to it. My knowing is sensory based. My sensory flames burn naturally. Language is not natural for me. Typing language is several energy transformations away from my core. Typing is gas on my fire of knowing. Like a good forest ranger, through lots of smutty trial and error, I learned to use this accelerant to control burns. Writing is very hard to do, especially when sensations are blazing. Daily scheduled typing allows one sensory fire to be processed at time. One fire is warm and illuminating. Multiple fires are chaotic and dangerous.

I know that being disguised as a poor thinker makes people curious about my abilities. "Can you read?" is a common question. I am not offended – okay, maybe a little – but here is the deal. I read well, one word at a time, if the font size is at least 18. However, I prefer to take a mental picture of the page, and file it so I may consider it and recall it at my leisure. The most efficient way for me to take in written information is to hear it. When I listen to audiobooks, my prized Great Teaching Courses, or someone reading aloud to me, I go into my half-shell. I pull my shirt over my head or, if I'm feeling unusually puritanical, I lower my head into my hands or a lap pillow so my vision will process only internal stimuli. I would simply close my eyes, but they do not reliably stay shut as "simply" is as uncommon in my design as fatal bowling injuries. I use all my energy to process heard words into visual representations, and file accordingly. If I have to read the words first, it requires a double translation from the twenty-six visual symbols to word chunks, and then again to visual scenes of meaning.

Once you understand how you think best, I recommend taking charge of your own enrichment and environment. I was at school but never in school. The mind is a beautiful place to be.

ZOOM: When did you start using Facilitated Communication?

B = 1992. I was nineteen years old and just returned from Syracuse, New York, where my parents met my mind for the first time in seventeen years. I'd had an early debut, but then, just before I turned two, my humanity went into hibernation.

Thinking ceased to build upon itself. That is when Barbara Ruth filled in for me and went into survival mode. Each moment was a confusing ambush, and she sought only to gulp the next breath of fleeting clarity. Words changed all that, and my parents bought those in upstate New York. It was a sweet purchase—two for one: words and a daughter with a mind fitted for external communication.

Some purchases change the world. I often write that I study history to know what is probable. I also study history to know what is possible. Consider the Louisiana Purchase and the consequent Lewis and Clark boundary mission, the "Corps of Discovery," they circumnavigated Great Falls. The Shoshone

Chief, Cameahwait, connected with his sister, Sacagawea, in Shoshone. She then spoke to her French-Canadian husband, Charbonneau, in Mandan (the language of a Sioux tribe). He then talked in French to Jusseaume (another interpreter), who communicated to Lewis and Clark in English. Gifts were exchanged and everybody got what they needed.

You will discover you can find a way to communicate. Then you too will exchange gifts and may achieve your destiny.

Zoom: How did you meet?

B = DD (Darling Dad) hired headhunters. Next thing I know, we had a family interview with a "highly recommended specialist." Turns out it was just baby doc SS in a flashy new sports car. I decided to keep her.

ZOOM: Did you both click right away, or did it take some time?

B = When typing takes so much time energy, it is wise to recycle. Please allow this excerpt from "I Might Be You" to set the stage…
     "Next, I was to get to know the smiling shrink. The following Monday, we went on a solo mission to Wendy's fast-food restaurant, where I conducted many experiments on the eager young shrink. First, repulsion – would she be able to withstand the public embarrassment of dining with a growling Neanderthal who devoured both portions of cow? She did so with a genuine smile. Next, fear – would she run from the unpredictable grabs by a larger, more menacing creature? No, the optimistically warped doctor misinterpreted my oafish assails as a friendly yet awkward closeness gesture. The most substantial test would take significantly more patience on my part. I will outlast her momentary interest by evading progress. I have outlasted the best of them. This well-intentioned do-gooder will soon retreat from my world, and I can resume my comfortable solitude.
     With any luck and decent manipulative creativity on my part, I will be safely tucked away in a posh home for institutionalized types by summer. That way, everybody wins. Mom and Dad are guilt-free and

can get some rest and golf a bit. The smiling shrink (SS) gains some well-needed experience with incorrigibles and gets paid for her troubles. And me – well, I can survive. No need to thrive. My mind is not a bad place to live. Who knows, I might even find another pot-smoking friend to help me pass the time.

Well, you could have knocked me over with a worm of floating light (like the ones seen drifting across one's visual field while staring into an overcast sky) when I felt myself enjoying her lively company so much.

A week into our work, our sessions were as welcome and revitalizing as that first gulp of air that I've finally sucked in after pushing through perfectly chlorinated water just prior to my lungs exploding from toying with living submerged permanently. I considered postponing my fancy institutional quest a while longer while I explored the depths of this new worker. This might amuse me for some time. The thing simply got out of hand.

Zoom: What is typical day like for you now?

B: Below is my typical IRL (in real life) schedule. PA = my personal attendant. I require twenty-four/seven care for safety and to stimulate the economy; Ian is my hottie personal trainer; Ed is an "autism specialist" (I am the real autism specialist, but I try not to get hung up on titles) who helps me practice independent typing and reads me what I choose to study that week; the unseen hero here is "Chill Time" where I refuel in my autism and mentally write what I plan to peck out the next day. Chill Time locations vary. A few of my favorites are: my front-yard swing, my living room with my feline roommate, Jane Eyre (especially when a fire is going – but a fan will suffice), or in bed under my trusty comforter.

Sunday
6:00 pm-8:00 am Monday   PA: Carol
9:00 am-noon Lois   Location: Pink House
TBA Date with Jerry
Monday

8:00 am-8:00 am Tuesday	PA: Brenda
9:00-noon Lois	Location: Pink House

Tuesday
8:00 am-5:00 pm	PA: Tere
5:00 pm-8:00 am Thursday	PA: Brenda
2:30 pm-3:00 pm Ian	Location: Ian's studio
4:00pm-5:30 pm Ed	Location: PEN

Wednesday
8:00 am-8:00 am Thursday	PA: Brenda
9:00 am-noon Lois	Location: Pink House
2:00 pm-2:45 pm Ian	Location: Ian's studio

Thursday
8:00 am-5:00 pm	PA: Carol
9:00 am-noon Lois	Location: Pink House
5:00 pm-3:00 pm Friday	PA: Tere
9:00 am- noon Lois	Location: Pink House
2:00 pm-2:45 pm Ian	Ian's studio

Friday
8:00 am-3:00 pm	PA: Tere
10:00 am- noon	Radio recording Location: PEN

Weekend PA: Carol

ZOOM: What made you decide to write your incredible book *I Might Be You: An Exploration of Autism and Connection,* and what lessons do you hope people take away from it?

B = SS keeps meticulous daily session notes from everyone who works with me. After filling a few binders of my "amazing transformations," we figured we should share what worked and what did not.

"There is hope for all" is the takeaway.

We are all teachers. For best results: Teach from the heart to the heart.

ZOOM: We love this quote of yours, "Autism is my Prism, not my Prison" – can you elaborate on that?

B: Yep. I plan on having t-shirts and mugs made with that lil' ditty. I am not alone in that truth, and I intend to do my fair share in making the appreciation of neurodiversity more common than juice stains in minivans.

Zoom: How did the radio show idea come about? And who came up with the name Loud Mute Radio?

B = I put the idea in SS's mind about ten years ago. Thoughts often take time to germinate, especially in ADHD heads.

L= That is funny. And Barb just told me that. I do remember when I was still at the University and working with Barb in my extra time that I started a "Radio Show Ideas" file. Then last August, I was pulling out of the neighborhood, driving Eli to school, and seemingly out of nowhere I said, "I am going to have a radio show." Eli and I both laughed at the apparent delusion of grandeur. A couple of weeks later, XXX Radio contacted my office to see if I was interested in having a radio show. (I know that sounds pornographic, but I am really just trying to redact their name. However, if I were going to do porno – radio would probably be the best format for me.) I ran the not-porno opportunity by Barb and she was enthusiastic. We thought about what to call it and laughed crazily right away. Simultaneously, Barb typed and I said – "LOUD MUTE RADIO!" The radio production company liked our ideas and sent us a contract proposal. When we saw that the lion's share of the ad revenue would go to XXX, we figured we'd better get a second opinion. So, we asked our marketing guru, Jennifer Ho-Dougatz, who co-owns Hangar Studios in NYC with her husband. Jen lit up and exclaimed that her hubby Chad Dougatz was JUST starting a podcast-and-radio-production service. We knew and adored

Chad from recording the audiobook. Chad sent us a counter proposal. And now Mule and Muse Productions owns LOUD MUTE RADIO, produced by Hangar Studios.

ZOOM: You have done quite a few radio shows now, covering a wide variety of topics: everything from depression to sexuality, financial planning, and finding your purpose... and everything in between. What have you learned about yourselves, or autism, or life in general, from interviewing all these great people?

B = I learned that SS's voice gets shaky when talking to famous people. I thought about firing her on the Andrew Solomon show, but he was so gracious and warm, she eventually got it together. I admire authenticity and perseverance. As he's famous for a reason, Dr. Andrew Solomon wrote, "The worst mistake anyone can make is to perceive anyone else as lesser."

L = I too find authentic and driven people fascinating and attractive. We highlight folks who are excited about what they do. Barb is the pattern connoisseur, but even I notice – across the board, these people are internally motivated and have optimistic mindsets. That is not to say that they don't feel pain, fear, or depression – but they make the best out of situations and drive on. Perhaps what inspires me the most is how generous these great people are with what they have learned.

Zoom: What or who is your biggest influence in life?

B = My parents. Smother and DD are my set. One could not ask for a more sagacious or supportive board of trustees.

Lois = My strong, strong wife Ty's unwavering support frees me to be as bold as I dare. I can't imagine a more fun, passionate, and supportive marriage. And I dreamed all my life of being a Mom. My son, Eli (now fifteen), balances me (his prefrontal cortex works better than mine). Eli consistently motivates me to give my best. I try never to take these unprecedented loves for granted. Barb and I clearly enjoy working with each other and our families.

B = Plus, nepotism is cost effective.

L = Yes, you will hear Smother, Jerry, Eli, and Ty on many shows. A show featuring Barb's Dad is in the works.

ZOOM: What advice do you give to parents? What about to the other autistic individuals out there?

B = Getting my book is a good start. If you can't afford a book, my court will provide one for you.

Lois = I am learning that "Experts Become Experts by Listening" (I stole that line from Jess Wilson's "Diary of a Mom" Blog.) Listen for strengths, and then build on those. For example, I learned that Barb has a powerful imagination. That is a gift. Imagination is the first step in solving every problem. So, Barb makes a terrific business partner. I am more likely to get bitten; but I am also more likely to get thoroughly considered possibilities, and her brutally honest opinion.

ZOOM: What's next for Mule and Muse Productions?

Barb = SS, it's time to advertise.

Lois = This fall, we will release another book.

Barb = Only four years this time. The last one took ten years. We may have to update my IEP.

Lois = The title is *Neurodiversity: A Humorous and Practical Guide to Living with ADHD, Anxiety, Autism, Dyslexia, The Gays, and Everyone Else.*

Barb = SS has more of those conditions than me so I will play the "normal" this round like she has been playing the mostly non-verbal in this interview.

Zoom: Just for fun: Coffee or Tea?

B = Tea, sweet B

L= Coffee with a comical amount of cream and sugar. It's hard to watch – rather like Robin Williams during his cocaine phase, but maybe with a little less body hair.

B = Not much less. I can't see well – I know I'm at work each morning when I hear her heart race.

Zoom: Dog or Cat?

B = My lovely roommate, Jane Eyre, marked "cat" on her application. Does that count?

L = Love dogs! We have two: A Papillon, named Britain, and Beagle – his given name is Matthew, but everybody just calls him Beagle.

B = That is not what I call him when he bays at 6 am.

L = Yes, Beagle is adjusting to city life. I would call them rescue dogs, but that makes us sound like we heroically fought bad guys and fires, dramatically whisking them from the jaws of death. Really, we just looked at cute dogs on line and went to the shelter with a check.

Zoom: Cake or Ice Cream?

Barb = Yes please. Carb lover b

Lois = Sweets do not interest me much, except during a certain time of the month.

Barb = See? Stupidly honest. More refined b

Zoom: Mountains or Beach?

B = I cherish both. One view is not better than the other – just different.

L = Barb typed that she is an observer and I am a participant. I choose both also. Many of the perfect moments in my life were swimming in mountain streams, snowboarding and skiing, or surfing. For me, the bliss comes from sharing the wave or moment with those I adore. Lucky for me Ty, Eli, and my dear friends are happy to join in the fun.

Zoom: Movies or Reading?

B = Since I am not yet in the movie business, I recommend reading.

L = Audiobooks at double speed.

Zoom: And last but not least, if you could have any super power, what would it be and why?

Barb = Telepathy… (I am mentally telling you why right now).

Lois = Teleportation, because it is efficient – and even more cost effective than nepotism.

Addendum to Dyslexia Chapter: Demonstrating the Connection Step to "Best Practices"

Observation One = 9-10:30 am

*On this day, to monitor issues with attention, I noted Ava's "On Task" behaviors on the minute mark during each 5-minute trial compared to another randomly selected peer. Ava was constantly wiggly but remained in her seat and appeared attentive for 85% of the time. This was not statistically different from her peers. When Ava did get off task it was non-disruptive. For example, she would simply play with the erasers in her desk. [It is important to consider attention issues when evaluating dyslexia, in order not to confuse the two and be more specific with appropriate recommendations. Ben Foss reports, in *The Dyslexia Empowerment Plan: A Blueprint for Renewing Your Child's Confidence and Love of Learning*, "40 percent of people from ADHD are also from Dyslexia, though the opposite is not the case, as there are more dyslexic people than ADHD folks." Foss' book, TED talk, and web site "Headstrong Nation" are also great resources. He is dyslexic himself, and invented the Intel Reader, a mobile device that takes pictures of text and recites it aloud. Plus, Foss is co-founder of Integration Ventures, a venture-capital firm created to invest in dyslexic entrepreneurs.]

9-9:10 am Consultation with Principal and Teacher. Primary concerns are the lack of progress in reading, writing, and spelling. Ava's academic performance is last in her class of 43 and the "gap is noticeable and growing." Some behavioral concerns were noted as well: "me first" mentality and lack of perseverance and effort on difficult cognitive tasks.

Ava sat in the front row and was eager to participate, and raised her hand often when she knew the answer. At 9:21 the level of "big" words on the spelling white board seemed to surpass her ability and speed, and Ava no longer shot up her hand. She spent her efforts erasing her writing to match the correct words on the white board. Mrs. Teacher corrected Ava discreetly at 9:26, but also quietly prompted 3 other students in similar ways. The environment was energetic and collaborative. Mrs. Teacher was entertaining, and used praise and attention well to keep the students engaged and actively participating in the 3 activities I observed during this time block.

The first activity was chain spelling, where students were called upon to make new words on the white board while Mrs. Teacher simultaneously reviewed spelling rules conversationally. Good control and lots of positive feedback. The students contributed and were often asked follow-up questions. Ava seemed to enjoy this activity and was very involved at first, but when the words got larger she became silent and played with her desk erasers.

The next exercise was math. The students were given a multi-step math word problem with written directions. The class was paired up into partners. Elle [name also changed for privacy and dyslexic ease... yay palindromes] was Ava's partner. I again observed Ava to start eagerly with her partner on the first two questions on the worksheet, but as the math problems became more complex, Elle took charge and Ava simply wrote down the answers. This became obvious to all when the activity was complete, and each group told the class how they arrived at their answers. Ava was unable to describe how they got these answers:

1. $93 divided by 2
2. How many $10 bills did each person get?
3. How many $1 bills did each person get?
4. How many cents did each person get?
5. How much money total did each person get?

Elle was able to share how each answer was derived.

The next activity was also to be done in pairs. The students were given magazines and asked to find:

1. One homophone
2. One contraction
3. One word with the "ah" sound
4. One proper noun and
5. One word that has the spelling pattern "ear."

Bob was Ava's partner. Ava seemed to really enjoy the social aspect of working with Bob and stood making happy dance moves for the most of their working time, but she was attentive and contributed the consonant blend, and cheered when he found the other items.

[A tender cherub in that class politely asked me "What does an "ear" pattern word sound like? I smiled and told him honestly, "I am not sure." I am no longer embarrassed about what I don't know: in fact, I use it to fuel my curiosity. A few years ago, when I started a private practice, Psychoeducational Network, I knew we wanted to offer empirically based, state-of-the-art reading therapy. Clearly, that was not my specialty, but I like to have a basic understanding of all parts of the company, so I signed up for Lindamood-Bell reading-therapist training in "Visualizing and Verbalization" for language comprehension and thinking; and "Seeing Stars" for phonemic awareness, reading, and spelling. This was a weeklong 8 am to 5 pm workshop with a group of about twenty educators at our local, overly air-conditioned Holiday Inn. I was able to hang just fine in the "Visualizing and Verbalization" training. But, "Seeing Stars" was difficult – very difficult. The seasoned instructor quickly noticed my Ava-like class participation and graciously did not call on me for things like nonsense-word pronunciations and other differentiating "phonemes" answers. After class, she graciously gave me additional materials designed to help dyslexics (for free). Later, I invited her to dinner at our Pink House and learned even more about what reading therapists do. Now I have a greater understanding about reading and reading therapy, but more importantly, I am better able to hire excellent reading therapists.

As Brian Grazer promotes in his book, *A Curious Mind: The Secret to a Bigger Life*, curiosity gives you power and can help you conquer fear and do what is hard and rewarding. Grazer himself did not write his best-selling book – he spoke it to a ghostwriter, which is not as spooky as it sounds. In fact, it is smart. Grazer is dyslexic and spends his time on what he excels in, and artfully delegates the rest. Grazer is a busy, big-time Hollywood producer responsible for such blockbusters as *Apollo 13, The Grinch, Frost/Nixon, J. Edgar, Night Shift, Splash,* and *A Beautiful Mind*, as well as a bunch of successful

TV series. Grazer even had another guy read aloud the audiobook. It is still his work, so Grazer gets the big bucks – and gets to tell Oprah all about it. Here is a Grazer quote I replayed on my iTunes audiobook five times, at regular speed, so I could re-tell it exactly: "I protect that part of myself, the part that is not afraid to seem briefly ignorant. Not knowing the answer opens up the world as long as you don't try to hide what you do not know. I try to never be self-conscious about not knowing."]

Observation Two 1:30-3 pm

Again on this day, no behavioral or attention problems were observed. Ava had two good days. It should be noted, the observer effect may account for improved behavior for all students. She is always moving, but was cooperative and engaged. Ava seemed happy and interested. But her self-awareness of her deficits is obvious. She was the only one to cover her writing work in science class both times, as I walked around the room looking at everyone's letter to an upcoming third grader. This shame is counterproductive and may lead to academic dishonesty and low self-esteem. Ava needs to understand more about her differences so she can use her considerable strengths to motivate her to do the hard work needed to improve her weaknesses.

1:30-1:40 = Observation and consultation in P.E. with Coach A and Coach B. Both reported that Ava has high athleticism, is very competitive, and plays hard. They confirmed Ava has some difficulty with complex instructions and often insists on "her way." Ava played the game with gusto and clearly enjoyed it. She also appeared happy and attentive as the Coaches let several children come to the front and tell jokes to both classes before they returned to the classroom. This was a very supportive and kind environment. I observed the PE teachers to call each student by name and often took time to talk patiently with individual children. The Coaches got the children's attention with a playful and productive "beep beep response." Ava had two private but seemingly positive conversations with Coach B.

1:40-2:40 = Observation and consultation in science class. This was a calm, confident class where Mrs. M quietly got and maintained the children's attention with a peaceful voice, and interesting and often unexpected content. If some students began to get distracted, Mrs. M would say something like "clap if you can hear me." The class was well behaved, and Ava smiled often and appeared interested for the duration. Mrs. M reiterated Ava's problems with her "me first" attitude, but was mostly concerned about Ava's significant reading, writing, and spelling delays. I observed these deficits on the in-class writing assignment. Ava's was significantly less advanced, in every way, than her peers.

2:45-3 pm = Observation and another brief consultation with Principal and main teacher. I see Ava benefiting from a great deal of immediate and positive attention, patience, and supportive peers at this time. The School's small student-teacher ratio, impressively nurturing and professional staff, and multi-sensorial learning activities are helpful. These elements should be part of the educational options considered.

Below are some educational options that we may wish to discuss to see what is the best fit for Ava at this time. After discussing the pros and cons of these options and more, I suggest we educate Ava on the situation and deal with the decision in a collaborative, problem-solving approach, so that she is empowered and takes more responsibility for making the consistent hard work needed to improve her weaknesses.

[RECOMMENDATIONS omitted. I am not including the specific recommendations for Ava because

1. they are related to the specifics of her school and
2. the solutions for this family are revealed in general terms later in the chapter.]

In considering all placement options, I recommend including the following priorities:

*Build on Ava's considerable strengths to grow her self-confidence and interest in learning.

*Help Ava understand how her mind works, including the unique specialties about how dyslexic minds function. (I am happy to discuss the topic with Ava, or she may enjoy listening to and discussing the audiobook version of Thomas Armstrong's brief chapter on Dyslexia. She may also benefit from watching the hour-long documentary called "The Big Picture: Rethinking Dyslexia.")

*Remediation of Ava's weakness is important, but it is crucial to make her reading therapy as fun and relevant to her interests and strengths as possible, to improve her motivation and rate of progression.

Thank you. I look forward to working with you all to help find the best educational opportunities for Ava.

Lois Prislovsky

These are the steps Ava went through:

1. The school asked her parents to get a psychoeducational assessment to better understand Ava's strengths and weaknesses, and to see what can be done about her performing well below grade level in reading, spelling, and writing.
2. A licensed school psychologist at PEN, Dr. Stephanie Carroll, conducted a full psychoeducational assessment over two days of testing. (This involved a full IQ and achievement report along with specific diagnostics for ADHD and dyslexia.)
3. Dr. Carroll shared and discussed her findings regarding Ava's dyslexia profile with her parents, and shared the report with The School.
4. After reading Dr. Carroll's full assessment, I observed Ava in class on two separate days to see both morning and afternoon performance. (The purpose of this was to gain more information about what types of support would be best for Ava.)
5. My observation report, with recommendations and a variety of schooling options, was discussed with Ava's parents. At this

time, I got on the same page with what the parents thought would work best for their family. The next step was to meet with the school and work out a mutually agreeable plan.

6. Ava's parents and I met with school principal, primary teacher, and teacher's aide (who helps administer pull-out support and technology accommodations). All parties found that the psychoeducational assessment and observation report made sense, and were in agreement about the support and accommodations planned.

7. Next I met with Ava and her parents to explain dyslexia, and the strengths and challenges associated with her style of thinking. Our intent was to help Ava drop the shame and begin to embrace her differences, along with starting to consider the hard work she will need to do over the summer and during the school year to strengthen her weaknesses. The fun technology accommodations were also discussed. Ava was very open and interested in the discussion and was clearly relieved to know why she struggled. She was particularly excited about the iPad she will get to use to help her dictate her writing, the text-to-speech converter to let her hear what she needs to read, and keyboarding software to help her quickly navigate the ever-improving software technology available for dyslexic learners. We were careful to structure this meeting as a collaborative problem-solving approach, so that Ava was actively being heard and taking ownership of her growth.

8. In this next step, Ava, her Mom, and I met for the first 30 minutes of the session to see if any anxiety or other concerns needed addressing before moving forward. All was good. For the second half of the session, Ava was introduced to her PEN reading therapist, Katie. They got to know each other, and talked about Ava's interests, in order to find alluring topics for reading-therapy work. The three agreed on a weekly schedule for summer support and a plan that would continue in the school year.

9. An ice cream social was the next step. SKREEECH! What? Yes, the principal and teachers suggested this at the meeting

where we all agreed on a plan of action. Ice cream socials are not typically part of the services we coordinate at PEN, but…

[I was thinking about how odd this step was, and whether or not to include it, when I heard "bzeep" then "bzeep… bzeep," (the sound my muted iPhone makes when I get new email if the inbox is left open – which is never open when I am writing as I try to keep distractions to a minimum). Happy for a little distraction, I checked my email. It contained three new emails about the joyous successes in Ava's ice cream social. Dear readers, that is the way the universe I love to live in works.]

And yes… it was June – this principal and these teachers were out for the summer and were not being paid for this.

Wow! What a compassionate and supportive team. Best practice? Yes, I think so! When everyone's intent is the best interest of the child, growth is imminent. I am thrilled to be a part of this family's solutions.

10. **Step 10 is to strive toward being part of solutions where everyone's intent is the best interest of the child – and thus Best Practice.**

Email chain from Ava's mom to the principal, teacher, teacher's aide, school counselor, PEN's reading therapist, and me (collectively known as Team Ava).

Email from Ava's mom to Team Ava:

"I just want to take a minute to say, 'Thank you!' My husband and I were SHOCKED when Ava took things so well. I think that we stressed and worried for months about this, when in reality, Ava took it all in stride. It was a telltale sign when she commented on how easy her summer

packet was this year. When we met with Lois, we really stressed the positives for Ava and she agreed. (Although her first question was, 'So, I will skip fourth grade the next year...' haha!) She has told several of her close friends, and they have been kind and excited for her, which I think has helped.
Thank you for taking Ava for ice cream yesterday! She truly enjoyed it and has been looking forward to it!

We are so excited about her future, and can't wait to see how the year plays out."

This email is from the principal to Team Ava.

"Our ice cream meeting with Ava was a wonderful treat on Wednesday! Ava was so confident and thoughtful, and just seemed to be happy all around.

It was interesting when I asked her a few things:
*I showed her (a visual of) how she was one of the youngest in last year's class and how now she would be one of the oldest (but not THE oldest); she blurted out "Yeah, I don't like that. I'm glad to be older... like Bob."
*She also shared that it will be nice not to be in class with a boy she has had difficulty with through the years (competitive, and they seem to push one another's buttons).
*I asked her how she felt about the work, and if it would be too easy or a relief – she quickly said that she was relieved that the work would not be as hard.
*We discussed how sometimes a "load can be lifted off your shoulders," and she said that was exactly how she was feeling.

We also discussed strategies if anyone says anything to her about being in third grade again this year. We role-played, and she seemed comfortable and okay with how to handle it if it comes up.

She was very excited to be a reading buddy to a kindergartener again, too.

She did make a class-list request [friend's name redacted] – and I will work on that combination. :)

Her questions were very thoughtful, and as Mrs. Teacher shared, many of them related to the iPad.

I have communicated with Katie [PEN's reading therapist] and we have Ava's schedule blocked off at school (Mon, Wed, Thur 1:40-2:40 each week), and Katie and I have an orientation meeting set up to familiarize her with the school (Tuesday, August 4 @ 11:30). The Lindamood-Bell books and materials have been given to [teacher's aide at school] and [Ava's mom].

I felt so at peace, and confident that this plan is going to boost Ava into a new place academically and socially.

Thank you to the [family] and Lois for setting Ava up for success in the earlier June meetings. You did an excellent job – because Ava has responded so well!"

This email was from Ava's primary teacher to Team Ava.

"It was great to see Ava today. Mrs. Principal and I both agreed that she looked more mature and confident, and also very at ease. She mostly had questions about her iPad. She seemed at peace with repeating third grade, she said she liked the idea of having me as a teacher again, she requested that [friend] be in her class, and she told us about her summer trip and some things she has been doing. We answered her questions about not going to science and, on some days, Spanish, and she was very okay with that. We had a good, fun conversation. [Since Ava will repeat third grade and will know how all the interactive science experiments turn out, we decided to use Science class as a time for Ava to have reading therapy during the school day, so that she can have her afternoons to pursue and enjoy her many extracurricular activities where she excels – building on her strengths.]

Please let me know if I can do anything over the summer to help Ava. Mrs. Principal and I will meet soon to knock out the details of Ava's schedule and how that will all be organized, and we will have all of that ready for you before school starts.

Again, I feel the meeting was great. I know I felt really good about how Ava seemed to be coping with this change."

Bibliography

Armstrong, Thomas. *The Power of Neurodiversity: Unleashing the Advantages of Your Differently Wired Brain*. Cambridge, MA: Da Capo Lifelong, 2011. Print.

Armstrong, Thomas. *Neurodiversity: Discovering the Extraordinary Gifts of Autism, ADHD, Dyslexia, and Other Brain Differences*. Cambridge, MA: Da Capo Lifelong, 2010. Print.

Brown, C. Brené. *The Gifts of Imperfection: Let Go of Who You Think You're Supposed to Be and Embrace Who You Are*. Center City, MN: Hazelden, 2010. Print.

Chittister, Joan. *Following the Path: The Search for a Life of Passion, Purpose, and Joy*. New York: Image, 2012. Print.

Chopra, Deepak. *The Seven Spiritual Laws of Success: A Practical Guide to the Fulfillment of Your Dreams*. San Rafael, CA: Amber-Allen Pub., 1994. Print.

Cuddy, A. (2012, June) Your body language shapes who you are [Video file] Retrieved from http://www.ted.com/talks/ amy_cuddy_your_body_language_shapes_who_you_are?langu age=en

Davis, Ronald D., and Eldon M. Braun. *The Gift of Dyslexia: Why Some of the Smartest People Can't Read... and How They Can Learn*. Perigee Books, 2010. Print.

Dweck, Carol S. *Mindset: The New Psychology of Success*. New York: Random House, 2007. Print.

Eide, Brock, and Fernette Eide. *The Dyslexic Advantage: Unlocking the Hidden Potential of the Dyslexic Brain*. New York: Hudson Street, 2011. Print.

Ellis, Albert. *How to Control Your Anxiety Before It Controls You.* Secaucus, NJ: Carol Pub. Group, 1998. Print.

Elmore, Tim. *Artificial Maturity: Helping Kids Meet the Challenge of Becoming Authentic Adults.* San Francisco: Jossey-Bass, 2012. Print.

Endow, Judy. "Is Autism a Disability or a Difference." *Oilbean.* Oilbean, n.d. Web. 20 Jan. 2016. <http://ollibean.com/2014/06/20/autism-disability-difference/>.

Ferrucci, Piero. *The Power of Kindness: The Unexpected Benefits of Leading a Compassionate Life.* New York: J.P. Tarcher/Penguin, 2006. Print.

Foss, Ben (2014, June 12). Choose Strength, not Shame. [Video file] Retrieved from http://tedxtalks.ted.com/video/Choose-Strength-not-Shame-Ben-F

Foss, Ben. *The Dyslexia Empowerment Plan: A Blueprint for Renewing Your Child's Confidence and Love of Learning.* New York: Ballantine, 2013. Print.

Frankl, Viktor E. *Man's Search for Meaning.* Boston: Beacon, 2006. Print.

Gabriel, Rachael E. *Reading's Non-Negotiables: Elements of Effective Reading Instruction.* Plymouth: Rowman & Littlefield, 2013. Print.

Gabriel, Rachael E., and Jessica Nina Lester. *Performances of Research: Critical Issues in K-12 Education.* New York: Peter Lang, 2013. Print.

Gladwell, Malcolm. *David and Goliath: Underdogs, Misfits, and the Art of Battling Giants.* New York: Hachette Book Group, 2013. Print.

Grandin, Temple, and Richard Panek. *The Autistic Brain: Helping Different Kinds of Minds Succeed.* New York: Houghton Mifflin Harcourt, 2013. Print.

Grandin, Temple, and Sean Barron. *The Unwritten Rules of Social Relationships: Decoding Social Mysteries Through the Unique Perspective of Autism.* Arlington, TX: Future Horizons, 2005. Print.

Grandin, Temple. *Thinking in Pictures: My Life with Autism.* New York: Doubleday, 1995. Print.

Grazer, Brian, and Charles Fishman. *A Curious Mind: The Secret to a Bigger Life.* New York: Simon & Schuster, 2015. Print.

Greene, Ross W. *The Explosive Child: A New Approach for Understanding and Parenting Easily Frustrated, "Chronically Inflexible" Children.* New York: HarperCollins, 1998. Print.

Hallowell, Edward M. *Driven to Distraction at Work: How to Focus and Be More Productive.* Boston: Harvard Business School, 2015. Print.

Hallowell, Edward M., and John J. Ratey. *Driven to Distraction: Recognizing and Coping with Attention Deficit Disorder from Childhood through Adulthood.* New York: Simon & Schuster, 1995. Print.

Hạnh, Thich Nhat. *The Art of Communicating.* New York: HarperCollins, 2013. Print.

Hạnh, Thich Nhat, and Melvin McLeod. *The Pocket Thich Nhat Hanh.* Massachusetts: Shambhala Publications, 2012. Print.

Hawking, Stephen, and Leonard Mlodinow. *The Grand Design.* New York: Bantam, 2010. Print.

Hay, Louise L., and Mona Lisa Schulz. *All Is Well: Heal Your Body with Medicine, Affirmations, and Intuition.* New York: Hay House, 2013. Print.

Higashida, Naoki. *The Reason I Jump: The Inner Voice of a Thirteen-Year-Old Boy With Autism.* New York: Random House, 2013. Print.

Hoff, Benjamin. *The Tao of Pooh.* New York, NY: Penguin, 1983. Print.

Johnson, Crockett. *Harold and the Purple Crayon.* New York: HarperCollins, 1958. Print.

Kennedy, Diane M., Rebecca S. Banks, and Temple Grandin. *Bright Not Broken: Gifted Kids, ADHD, and Autism.* San Francisco: Jossey-Bass, 2011. Print.

Kent, Jack. Socks for Supper. New York: Parents Magazine Press, 1978. Print.

Leahy, Robert L. *Anxiety Free: Unravel Your Fears Before They Unravel You.* Carlsbad, CA: Hay House, 2009. Print.

McGonigal, K. (2013, June) How to make stress your friend [Video file] Retrieved from http://www.ted.com/talks/kelly_mcgonigal _how_to_make_stress_your_friend?language=en

Moss, Haley. *Middle School – The Stuff Nobody Tells You About: A Teenage Girl with ASD Shares Her Experiences.* Kansas: Autism Asperger, 2010. Print.

Nepo, Mark. *Seven Thousand Ways to Listen: Staying Close to What Is Sacred.* New York: Free, 2012. Print.

Nepo, Mark. *The Book of Awakening: Having the Life You Want by Being Present to the Life You Have.* Berkeley, CA: Conari, 2000. Print.

Palmer, Parker J. *Let Your Life Speak: Listening for the Voice of Vocation*. San Francisco: Jossey-Bass, 1999. Print.

Pirsig, Robert M. *Zen and the Art of Motorcycle Maintenance: An Inquiry into Values*. New York: Morrow, 1974. Print.

Rankin, Lissa. *The Fear Cure: Cultivating Courage as Medicine for the Body, Mind, and Soul*. New York: Hay House, 2015. Print.

Rentenbach, Barb, and Lois Prislovsky. *I Might Be You: An Exploration of Autism and Connection*. Knoxville, TN: Mule and Muse Productions, 2012. Print.

Robinson, Ken, and Lou Aronica. *Finding Your Element: How to Discover Your Talents and Passions and Transform Your Life*. New York: Penguin Group, 2013. Print.

Rossman, Martin L. *The Worry Solution: Using Breakthrough Brain Science to Turn Stress and Anxiety into Confidence and Happiness*. New York: Crown Archetype, 2010. Print.

Shaywitz, Sally E. *Overcoming Dyslexia: A New and Complete Science-Based Program for Reading Problems at Any Level*. New York: A.A. Knopf, 2003. Print.

Siegel, Daniel J. *Brainstorm: The Power and Purpose of the Teenage Brain*. New York: Penguin Group, 2013. Print.

Siegel, Daniel J. *The Developing Mind: Toward a Neurobiology of Interpersonal Experience*. New York: Guilford, 1999. Print.

Silberman, Steve: *NeuroTribes: The Legacy of Autism and the Future of Neurodiversity*. New York: Avery, 2015. Print.

Solomon, Andrew. "The Middle of Things: Advice for Young Writers - The New Yorker." *The New Yorker*. The New Yorker, 11 Mar. 2015. Web. 20 Jan. 2016. <http://www.newyorker.com/books/page-turner/the-middle-of-things-advice-for-young-writers>.

Solomon, Andrew. "Searching for Answers After Sandy Hook - The New Yorker." *The New Yorker*. The New Yorker, 17 Mar. 2014. Web. 20 Jan. 2016. <http://www.newyorker.com/magazine/2014/03/17/the-reckoning>.

Solomon, Andrew. *Far from the Tree: Parents, Children and the Search for Identity*. New York: Scribner, 2012. Print.

Solomon, Andrew. *The Noonday Demon: An Atlas of Depression*. New York: Scribner, 2001. Print.

Stillman, William. *The Soul of Autism: Looking beyond Labels to Unveil Spiritual Secrets of the Heart Savants*. Franklin Lakes, NJ: New Page, 2008. Print.

Sunday, T. (2015, June 12) Dyslexia 2.0: The Gift of Innovation & Entrepreneurial Mind [Video file] Retrieved from http://tedxtalks.ted.com/video/Dyslexia-2-0-The-Gift-of-Innova

Suskind, Ron. *Life, Animated: A Story of Sidekicks, Heroes, and Autism*. Glendale: Kingswell, 2014. Print.

Tammet, Daniel. *Born on a Blue Day: Inside the Extraordinary Mind of an Autistic Savant: A Memoir*. New York: Free, 2007. Print.

Tsabary, Shefali. *The Conscious Parent: Transforming Ourselves, Empowering Our Children*. Vancouver: Namaste Pub., 2010. Print.

Uddin, Lucina Q., Ph.D. "Study Examines Brain Network Connectivity in Children with Autism Spectrum Disorder." *The JAMA Network* (n.d.): n. pag. *The JAMA Network*. The JAMA Network, 26 June 2013. Web. 16 Feb. 2016. <http://media.jamanetwork.com/news-item/study-examines-brain-network-connectivity-in-children-with-autism-spectrum-disorder/>.

Vonnegut, Mark. *The Eden Express: A Memoir of Insanity*. New York: Seven Stories, 2002. Print.

Walker, Nick. "What Is Autism?" *NEUROCOSMOPOLITANISM RSS*. NEUROCOSMOPOLITANISM RSS, 1 Mar. 2014. Web. 20 Jan. 2016. <http://neurocosmopolitanism.com/what-is-autism/>.

Weiss, Lynn. *Attention Deficit Disorder In Adults: Practical Help and Understanding*. Lanham: Taylor Trade, 1997. Print.

West, Thomas G. *In the Mind's Eye: Visual Thinkers, Gifted People with Dyslexia and Other Learning Difficulties, Computer Images, and the Ironies of Creativity*. Amherst, NY: Prometheus, 1997. Print.

Williams, Donna. *Everyday Heaven: Journeys Beyond the Stereotypes of Autism*. London: Jessica Kingsley, 2004. Print.

Williams, Donna. *Somebody Somewhere: Breaking Free from the World of Autism*. New York: Times Book, 1994. Print.

Williams, Donna. *Nobody Nowhere: The Extraordinary Autobiography of an Autistic*. New York: Times, 1992. Print.

Williams, Penny. "Can Neurofeedback Help Kids with ADHD Press the Restart Button?" *Healthlines RSS News*. Healthlines RSS News, 3 Feb. 2013. Web. 20 Jan. 2016. <https://www.healthline.com/health-news/can-neurofeedback-help-kids-with-adhd-020315>.

Wilson, Jess. "A Diary of a Mom." *A Diary of a Mom*. N.p., 11 Aug. 1999. Web. 15 Mar. 2015. <http://adiaryofamom.com/>.

Zakaria, Fareed. *The Post-American World: Release 2.0*. New York: W. W. Norton, 2011. Print.

CPSIA information can be obtained
at www.ICGtesting.com
Printed in the USA
LVOW02*1424250816
501845LV00001B/1/P